DEDICATION

For Esi – Esi & Pop Pop Forever

LVXXIII
to my crew for giving me a reason to embrace life
I love you always

My Parents
for heeding the call of the voices of your ancestors
Long live JLW and Sumbry Clans

Nyame Bekyre Family
1 for 1 Undisputed Champions

Omowale Malcom X
to our black star shining prince
thank you for your example of African manhood

Nana Kwame Agyei Akoto, Sankofaman
For all the Black people who will never touch African soil

RQQ to the Akwanbo 7
Friendship is Essential to the Soul

Editors:

Abena Makini Owusu
Maisha Hyman Sumbry

Contributing Authors:
Gabriel Ammah
Gbontwi Anyetei
S. Akosua Magee
Danny Damah
Amma Gyampo
Brenda Joyce
Obádélé Kambon
Ivy Prosper

Research Associates:
Richmiller Kwame Aboagye
Pascal Kwabla Ayanu
Bernard Atieku Boateng
Dora Abena Dzaka
Aikins Okwae Okulu

"When a person places the proper value on freedom, there is nothing under the sun that he will not do to acquire that freedom. Whenever you hear a man saying he wants freedom, but in the next breath he is going to tell you what he won't do to get it, or what he doesn't believe in doing in order to get it, he doesn't believe in freedom. A man who believes in freedom will do anything under the sun to acquire . . . or preserve his freedom."

- Omowale Malcolm X

TABLE OF CONTENTS

OUR JOURNEY 1

DEFINING YOUR PERSONAL WHY 9

WHY GHANA? 17

DEMOGRAPHICS: GHANA IS A COUNTRY 25

KNOW SOME HISTORY (SMALL SMALL) 35

    INTRODUCING GBONTWI ANYETEI 38

ALL BLACK PEOPLE LOOK ALIKE: ETHNICITY AND LANGUAGE 51

    INTRODUCING OBADELE BAKARI KAMBON, PH.D 52

CHOP LIFE: FOOD & DIET 75

HEALTH CARE: HOSPITALS & INSURANCE 81

EDUCATION: THEORY & PRACTICE 87

    INTRODUCING SHANNAN AKOSUA MAGEE 90

MANAGING YOUR PRIVILEGE, EXPECTATIONS & RELATIONSHIPS 105

HONORABLE & YOU: THE GOVERNMENT 117

    INTRODUCING DANNY DAMAH 125

MANAGING BANDS: MONEY & FINANCE 139

LIVING LEGAL: CITIZENSHIP, RESIDENCY & PERMITS 147

DIRTY GAMES: LAND, REAL ESTATE & RENTING 151

Introducing Gabriel Ammah 161

Managing Traffic: Business & Investment 169

Introducing Amma Gyampo 174
Introducing Brenda Joyce 182

Deeply Rooted: Tourism, Culture & Art 185

Endless Enjoyment: Nightlife & Entertainment . 193

Media & Messaging 197

Introducing Ivy Prosper 200

V8 vs. Everybody: Transportation 207

Shipping, Moving & Living 211

PREFACE

Shortly after being appointed as Director in 2017 at Diaspora Affairs, Office of the President (DAOOP), the government set out to engage with its Diaspora and the historical African community, a continuation of an initiative introduced by the previous NPP government in 2007. This initiative was known as The Joseph Project. Taking its name and inspiration from the Biblical Joseph, the initiative, reconciliatory in nature was to bring together African people fragmented as a result of our enslavement, ensuring Ghana was the beacon in this process of return on the continent. This was spearheaded by Former President H.E. John Agyekum with Hon. Jake Obetsebi Lamptey of blessed memory as Minister of Tourism and Diaspora Affairs.

In 2018, the President, H.E. Nana Addo Dankwa Akufo-Addo through the then Minister of Tourism Hon. Catherine Afeku reaffirmed the drive to engage the Diaspora. Through the executing agency, Ghana Tourism Agency, we began the discussions to promote our Tourism Industry while at the same time engaging the historical Diaspora.

As DAOOP pushed for policies to ensure a meaningful engagement, we were introduced to Diallo Sumbry of The Adinkra Group by the Ghana Tourism Authority. Through The Adinkra Group, the government established contact with the top magazine publication, Ebony, dedicated to celebrating Blackness. Here then, was the chance to communicate to a wider audience what we had been working on.

Later in 2018, with the formation of the Steering Committee for the Year of Return 2019 with Adinkra Group as partners, the committee leveraged Adinkra's network in the United States of America and as a result Adinkra was introduced to the Ghana

Ambassador to the USA leading to the commencement of the preparation for the international launch of the Year of Return 2019 in September, 2018 by H.E., the President.

We are limited by space to recount the success of the Year of Return, Ghana 2019 but it was through meaningful partnerships like what we had with the Adinkra Group and their Birthright Journeys which they hosted that contributed to the overall success.

Akwasi Awua Ababio
Director
Diaspora Affairs, Office of the President

Connect with DAOOP

FOREWORD

I am delighted to provide input into this book because I believe in the educative value of what this represents to the global African family. I met Diallo Sumbry in June 2017, through an introduction by Gina Paige of AfricanAncestry.com, on the fringes of the U.S.-Africa Business Summit organized by the Corporate Council on Africa in Washington DC. Then as in now, I was amazed at his passion for Africa and commitment to his roots. On the first day we met, we discussed working together and within six months, we had signed an MOU between the Ghana Tourism Authority (GTA) and his organization, The Adinkra Group, to collaborate in increasing tourism, business and investment in Ghana through various projects including the Back2Africa Tour and Heritage Documentary.

The signing of the MOU was part of our ongoing efforts at GTA to maximize exposure of Ghana as a destination of choice in the US market. Little did I envisage that; Diallo will so rapidly journey from being a Diasporan to becoming a citizen in the homeland. He has embraced our people, culture and heritage and rightly claimed his birthright as an African. We worked together on his Back 2 Africa projects, documentaries and as key actors on the steering committee of the Year of Return, Ghana 2019.

This guide is a bold attempt by Diallo, in providing a first-hand and practical testimony of how it is to "Return". This book can help all of us, African's home and those across the Atlantic, develop a shared understanding of our "different cultures". I call it Ghana 101 in that it offers a bit of everything that one needs to know in making the journey back.

This book is a must read for all and will become one of the testimonies and legacies of the Year of Return and the follow-up Beyond the Return projects. It is my prayer that through this, many more will heed the call and make that journey to Ghana to experience the country's culture, heritage, people and history. In the words of our President, H.E Nana Addo Dankwa Akufo-Addo, "We have to work together to make sure that never again will we allow a handful of people with superior technology to walk into Africa, seize our peoples and sell them into slavery".

This book will not just provide knowledge but touch lives and expand the frontiers of engagement.

God bless our homeland Ghana!

Akwasi Agyeman

CEO, Ghana Tourism Authority   **Visit Ghana**

INTRODUCTION

Thank you for purchasing A Smart Ghana Repatriation Guide, 1st Edition. Repatriation is defined as "the process of returning an asset, an item of symbolic value, or a person—voluntarily or forcibly—to its owner or their place of origin or citizenship." In this particular case, I am talking about the voluntary act of Black people returning to Africa – specifically Ghana.

This book is intended to be a comprehensive, practical and interactive resource for Black people (African-Americans, Black, Negro, Colored or however you personally identify as a person of African descent) who wish to either permanently relocate to Ghana at once, begin a multiple-year transition process to eventually fully integrate in Ghanaian society, or establish a second home in Ghana (#nomorewinters).

This book may also be useful for potential tourists, and those who seek to establish businesses or commercial partnerships with Ghanaians, though it is important to understand that this is not a Ghana Business or Tourism Guide.

Smart refers to the QR codes you will find throughout the book in each chapter that you can scan by simply opening the camera on your smartphone and focusing it on the QR code as you did with the cover on the book. You don't need to download an app or an external program. The QR codes are connected to videos, documents, reports, and real life information we hope you find useful. The QR codes are reviewed and updated quarterly if necessary.

I focus on African Americans because it's the only experience I have. Though our experiences are varied – generationally, geographically, educationally, and socioeconomically, we share the common fact that we are the direct descendants of kidnapped and enslaved Africans who served as the foundation on which the

Introduction

United States of America – "the most powerful nation on the planet" – was built.

As a whole race (notwithstanding our many subgroups) - African Americans –have, and continue to be, victims of overt, covert and systemic oppression, racism, bigotry, genocide, police brutality and abuse. This mistreatment has been intentionally designed to keep us stuck in cycles of despair, poverty, addiction, imprisonment, self-hate, self-destruction, and anything that has contributed to our historical and current fight to get white peoples' knees off our necks.

Again, this book is intended to be a resource. This is not a means to an end, but a single resource with what I believe to be some of the most essential topics (along with my personal experiences, anecdotes and useful tips) necessary for your move and successful integration into Ghanaian life. I'm eternally grateful for the special guest contributors for sharing their valuable experiences.

This guide is meant to be useful to both the historically and geographically astute and naive. Whether you've traveled to Ghana, other parts of Africa, or are a student of the world, this guide is meant to be a useful tool for you. It's designed to be as helpful to those on a budget who live modestly and have limited means as it is for those who have a little more room in their budget to live life fairly free from economic worry.

Likewise, the moderate or extreme baller can also find it useful. No matter your economic status, it is wise to take your time and - whenever possible - work with a trusted source on the ground.

If as you read through this guide and it sounds like I may be trying to talk you out of moving or relocating to Ghana, I am. And if I succeed, Ghana is not for you. Consider it a wild garden of roses with thorns. I am being as truthful and honest with you as I am with

Introduction

myself about my experiences and choices. I hope this book encourages, challenges, and excites your thought process and potential decision to move to Ghana. Surviving - let alone thriving - in Ghana can be an extra difficult task, and frankly, it may not be for you.

I represent a group of problem solvers, visionaries, doers, thinkers, builders and comrades from the diaspora who see Ghana and ultimately a unified Africa as a viable, realistic option for life and want to make their contribution. We're building bridges. We're re-connecting the diaspora. We're in the process of undoing what over hundreds of years of colonization and white terrorism has done to separate us. And while perfection doesn't exist in Ghana or anywhere in the world, Africa deserves repatriates whose missions are aligned and underscored with the spirit of collaboration and cohesiveness. We honestly don't need or want complainers.

Ideally, I want to reach people who can see nine generations ahead and are willing to plant seeds for their great, great, great grandchildren to enjoy the shade. If you also just want to buy a good book, add to your library, or support a brother without being connected to any of that real deep stuff I just wrote - that's cool too. In the words of Professor P. L. O. Lumumba:

"Your duty and my duty is to plant the tree in the knowledge that one generation plants a tree. Another generation waters the tree. Another generation prunes the tree. Another generation enjoys the shade. That is our duty." **Listen to the speech >>>>>>>>>>>>**

I cannot emphasize enough the importance of having a trusted confidant or network of like-minded individuals on the ground in Ghana. Having access to people who have constructed their own networks of individuals who are on the same wavelength, and who speak your language – literally and figuratively – will go a long way

Introduction

in making the transition to Ghana a much smoother, more positive experience. You will find this more valuable than anything else, even if just in parts. So if you have someone in mind- great! However, the tro tro ain't pulling off until it's full regardless so you still might as well read the whole book ☺.

This book is a valuable resource for everyone. I have learned a tremendous amount while writing this book, reading the special guests' contributions, and having ongoing conversations about repatriation. I am still learning from people every day. For those of you who have already moved or chosen to repatriate to Ghana, you'll blaze your own trails, write your own books and hopefully teach me and everyone else something along the way we haven't learned. I personally look forward to that! But if you've bought or borrowed it and read it anyway, thank you.

I'm forever grateful for the individuals and institutions, private and government, of Ghana who welcomed me into their fold. Again, thank you for your purchase. I look forward to your feedback, reviews, and conversations.

Introduction

Entrepreneur - Watch the Video >>>>>>

Uh, lies told to you

Through YouTubes and Hulus

Shows with no hues that look like you do

Black Twitter, what's that?

When Jack gets paid, do you?

For every one Gucci, support two FUBU's

Sippin' Crip-a-Cola

Consumer and a owner

'Til we all vertically integrated from the floor up

D'Ussé pour up

Sip Ace 'til I throw up

Like gang signs, 'cept I bang mines for both ya

Serial entrepreneur, we on our own

Stop sittin' around waitin' for folks to throw you a bone

If you can't buy the building, at least stock the shelf (word)

Then keep on stacking 'til you stocking for yourself, uh

See everything you place after black

Is too small a term to completely describe the act

Black nation, Black builder, Black entrepreneur

You in the presence of Black excellence and I'm on the board, Lord

- Hov (Jay Z)

Introduction

Follow the Oseadeeyo Kwasi Akuffo Foundation (OKWAF)

OUR JOURNEY

Our journey comes from the recognition that no man is an island. My family is with me at all times and while they haven't been able to make every trip and take part in every benchmark or turn, it remains our journey. I have never been alone on this journey and am comforted by the fact that I will never be. Our journey is just beginning.

It is important for me to note that I've been a professional, authentic, original Black African booty scratcher my whole life. My introduction to "Africa" and a "Pan African" worldview started from birth. I was African from the dirt. My parents raised me and my siblings in independent African centered institutions, and introduced to the breadth, depth, variety, and antiquity of African cultural traditions from the womb. In many ways my life prepared me for the work I am doing now.

Visit the Council of Independent Black Institutions (CIBI) >>>>>>>>>>>>>>>>>

I honestly can't say that I chose Ghana versus Ghana choosing me. I think we choose each other. You'll find a lot of people with that story. There's just something captivating about Ghana. Many have come for a visit and just stayed. It changed their life. Maybe it's the gold in the earth or the fufu. For the past few years, more often than not, I've been guided by faith - literally not knowing exactly why I was here until the last or next to last day of a trip - trying to piece it all together on airport coffee shop napkins, journals, and iPhone memos.

> *Faith is an oasis in the heart which will never be reached by the caravan of thinking. – Khalil Gilbran*

Senegal was my first African love in 1988. I had travelled back and forth often. My first time in Ghana was 2014. Many of my family

Our Journey

members and friends had been coming to Ghana for years and I was one of the last of the crew to make it. My first trip to Ghana was specifically to visit Nyame Bekyere – my current home village, which is located in the Akuapem North section of the Eastern Region of Ghana. I returned again to Ghana twice in 2016.

In 2017 Ghana officially changed the trajectory of my life. My good friend and business partner, Dr. Gina Paige of AfricanAncestry.com insisted that I meet Mr. Akwasi Agyeman, the CEO of the Ghana Tourism Authority. who was in town attending a conference in Washington, DC. It was at that meeting that I pitched the Back2Africa Festival. We eventually (6 months later) signed a memorandum of understanding (MOU) and developed a respected working and professional relationship that endures to this day.

<<<<<<Follow African Ancestry on Instagram

I brought two groups to Ghana in 2017 and my first large group of over 50 people with the Backyard Band for the first Back2Africa Festival in early 2018. It became apparent to me and my family, that Ghana was calling me home for a greater purpose.

With a successful partnership on the Back2Africa Festival in February 2018, I was able to successfully pitch and organize a short US ground tour by the Ghana Tourism Authority in March 2018 called Homecoming 2019 grounded by the introduction of H.R. 1242, 400 Years of African-American History Commission Act, the UN's in progress decade for people of African descent (2015 – 2024) and Bible's 400 year prophecy (Genesis 15:13) The purpose of this trip was for the heads of the Ghana Tourism Authority to hear from African Americans in the States that travel to Ghana and for them to share information about heritage tourism in Ghana. The tour covered three cities – Washington, DC, New York, and Chicago.

Our Journey

<<<<<Back2Africa Documentary trailer

Mr. Agyeman had mentioned a few times in our many conversations that I should meet a young man named Terry Oppong. Ahead of the tour, Terry and I connected through Instagram. We had only texted a bit back and forth but I reached out to him for partnership and he put together a powerful room in New York for the Ghana Tourism Authority. Terry Oppong is the real Ghana plug. His friendship and support with this and future initiatives would prove invaluable. He continues to be one of my most trusted friends on the ground in Ghana.

Connect with Terry Oppong>>>>>>>

In July 2018, the original Year of Return Steering Committee was formed. We were tasked with flushing out the concept of the Year of Return and creating the infrastructure that would manage it. Finding a brandable name that defined the concept was an important first step. The Steering Committee launched the Year of Return, Ghana 2019, in August 2018 at the National Theatre in Ghana during an Ebony Magazine delegation visit. The Year of Return was officially launched by H.E. President Nana Addo Dankwa Akufo Addo at the National Press Club in the U.S. on September 28, 2018. I remain humbled and honored to have been trusted to work with the Ghana Embassy and coordinate the launch in D.C.

Watch my remarks at the launch>>>>>

In late-2018, I secured my first apartment in the Asylum Down section of Accra. My landlord at the time, Gabriel Ammah, whom I now consider a brother, friend and construction mentor, is a contributing guest author. Having a safe, stable, and secure base from which to work and organize while in Ghana went a long way in my ability to work effectively and efficiently. Later that year, I was bestowed the honor of being named the first African American Tourism Ambassador of Ghana due to my work as a co-architect of the Year of Return. In 2019, I was selected to be Nkosuohene (Chief of Development) of Nyame Bekyre by the people and council of elders.

Nyame Bekyere is my spiritual home. It's the place I go to get centered, meditate and connect with powers beyond human capacity. Nyame Bekyere, its families, and the development of the community are extremely important to me. Nyame Bekyere is the site of a spiritual health resort for people of African descent slated to be fully completed by 2023. We have also partnered with the local Cocoa Board District to rehabilitate several thousand hectares of cocoa farmland and employ hundreds of local residents. My commitment to the youth and their education has also directed me to adopt the local school and erect the Niambi Inuka Sumbry Library and Technology Center. The Center is dedicated to the legacy of my younger sister, Niambi, whose work with youth prior to her passing in July 2017 was impactful and unfailing.

Help us complete the library>>>>>>>>>

I would be remiss not to mention my best friend, partner and brother Emerson Gibson – Spyda the DJ - who also passed away - February 14, 2017. Both his spirit and Niambi's have guided, pushed, compelled, and directed my energy along this journey. Both Niambi and Spyda were part of the Ghana Master Plan as it was coming to life. Their deaths have empowered me to live strong and still serve as an inspiration for me today. #Forever5 #Spydastrong

From 2017 – 2019 I met more people than I can remember. I was on automatic pilot and my ancestors wouldn't let me take a break.

Our Journey

They were riding me heavy and hard so I was just going where they cleared the path for me. The pandemic was perfect timing. I needed to research, write, breathe, sleep and really slow down to figure out exactly what I am doing in Ghana and ask myself if Ghana was the place for me.

Support the SpydaStrong Foundation>>>>>

As terrible as it was for the world and those who lost loved ones, jobs, their sanity and had their worlds turned upside down, the COVID-19 pandemic -just 3 months into 2020 - for me was a full blessing. More than anything, it forced me to slow down and provided the opportunity to reflect over the 2 - 3 years prior and focus on goals and objectives for the next 5 – 10 years.

In the relatively short time that I've been traveling back and forth to Ghana, we've provided the Birthright Journey experience to over 1.000 African Americans. And there is still so much more to be done, seen, and explored. There are so many exciting things to do and the landscape changes so quickly that it will really take a full committed lifetime to really experience all of Accra and greater Accra. I am no longer a tourist and have drawn that line.

Though I am comparatively young in the repatriation journey and have yet to permanently locate, I believe this offering is timely, valuable and necessary. I will never claim to know everything about Ghana or repatriation but I know what I know. Despite the fact that all Black people weren't kidnapped from Ghana and while some of us may find our actual roots in modern day Ghana and many of us will not, Ghana has remained a beacon of hope for the African in the diaspora longing to be home since its Independence.

As you will read very clearly in this book, *I am not suggesting that moving to Ghana is the answer for Black people who are tired of America.* I can't say that America's deep seated loathing and consistent attempts at genocide against Black people are good

Our Journey

enough reason alone to repatriate because America is still our home. Nor can I say the love I've grown to have for being "in Africa" and the feeling I get from the bottom of my feet through my spine to the top of my head is a good enough reason alone to repatriate. However, I have chosen not to be "stuck" anywhere. I've widened my perspective about life, living, existing, and being and I've decided that Africa is a much better place for me to live out the rest of my years, rebuild a foundation, give my energy, plant seeds in fertile soil and feed my prayers. I have very, very strong roots in America. My maternal and paternal families are both proof of our collective resilience and efforts that have built America. My maternal and paternal family have been able to trace their roots back to the 1700's so I am clear we built America and have unquestionable sweat equity in the corporation.

I also understand and accept my responsibility in my family and community to lead the way on this particular path, and help create a welcoming space for them when they are ready to make the move. I've been on my "Africa shizzle" for a while now and have been trying to figure out how to explain myself to myself first and then to others. I don't think moving to Africa is THE ANSWER. Nor do I think DIVORCING AMERICA is THE ANSWER. But I know how coming to Africa can reawaken a part of you that you may have never met. That will change you in a way you haven't been changed previously. And that will connect you in a way you haven't been connected previously. What I do think and know to an extent is that Black people - African Americans, specifically, are the lost tribe of the world and we will have to fight for belonging no matter where we are - America, Africa, Europe, Asia, South America, Australia or Antarctica.

I want Black people to know that we can choose our battleground. We can choose the best place to engage in a fight for a deeper belonging or proximity to God while we're on our physical mission. I chose Ghana because even though I still fight for belonging in

Our Journey

Ghana to an extent, I can at least be connected to the natural elements unfettered. I can grow my own food easily and inexpensively. I can live well with less. I can see and be surrounded by other Black people. I can help create tangible change. And more than anything else, as a Black man, I can live fully without my life being threatened for something as trivial as a traffic stop, dancing in the street or jogging. In Ghana, there is an overwhelming abundance of opportunity to create the life I want for myself and family while building a legacy that encompasses both my African and American composition.

I'm not interested in denouncing my American self or never returning to America because it's what makes me who I am. But I've been able to put my relationship with America in perspective – much like one who has reconciled their relationship with an abusive parent. I do not lean heavily on America to love me back as it will push back against me until I'm bent, cracked and broken to the point where I don't recognize myself. Most importantly, where I've allowed America and any geographical location to stand with me and my peace of mind. It's necessary internal work.

I have made and maintained some solid business and personal relationships in Ghana. I have also had to let a few go. Most importantly I've met some really dope people who have become friends with whom I plan to maintain a lifelong relationship. These are cherished individuals who've opened a door, showed me a new spot, introduced me to a contact, or offered me a million dollars' worth of game here and have been the greatest benefit to my personal journey so far. Afterall, friendship is essential to the soul.

Take note of your journey and what led you to this place. Where did you first learn to love Africa and decide that you were ok with being African? Take note of your journey.

Our Journey

Follow The Adinkra Group on Facebook

Slide in The Adinkra Group DMs on Instagram

Follow me (I don't check DMs often)

DEFINING YOUR PERSONAL WHY

- So you think you want to move to Africa?
- And you want to move to Ghana?
- Or do you want to move out of America?
- And Ghana seems like the next best place?
- Or does it all sound & feel the same?
- Do You have a deep longing? Is Ghana is calling you?
- Are you regular sure? Or are you sure sure?
- You visited & had such a great time over your stay?
- You got stuck during COVID?
- The social media posts throughout the Year of Return?
- You met a bae & fell in love?
- Ghana Jollof? Fufu? Banku & Tilapia? Pineapples?
- Are you regular sure? Or are you sure sure?
- The strong men? You met Dexter?
- The beautiful, shapely women? You met Sunshine?
- Maybe it's the currency exchange rate?
- Opportunity? Business? Investment? You see a flip?
- The weather? It is very nice in Ghana most of the year.
- You met some good people & talk every day on WhatsApp?
- You stopped loving the things you love about America?
- Your family supports you? Or nah but you'll show them?
- Are you Married? Do You have Children? Are you looking?

Get help defining your why>>>>>>>>>>

Asking yourself if you're sure, and discovering your why, will serve as the foundations of discovering your reason for moving. It will serve you both ways - whether you've thought about it and discovered why you will move or after reading this book and doing your own research - why you will stay. Your WHY should be composed of a multitude of reasons

Defining Your Personal Why

that encompass your full range of available human elements - emotional, physical, psychological, financial, spiritual, mental, intellectual, historical, familial and social.

The repeated question "are you sure?" is not because I am suggesting you need to be sure. Surety is relative and constantly changing based on the situation and environment. Most of us were pretty sure, despite racism, that America was the safest and best place to be before COVID-19 exposed it like the number of police murders that have surfaced via cell phone recordings. Some of us are still sure. The question is also one that I've found myself asking in Ghana – "Are you sure?"

Your WHY will encompass the cornerstone of your personal or family mission and vision. It's what you fall back on when you become unsure of everything. It's what keeps you going when you have a setback. It's what keeps you focused and committed when you start missing American fast food. Or when you start missing TJ Maxx, Marshalls, Walmart, Target, and Whole Foods. Or when you're stuck in traffic on the motorway in Ghana. Or when the lights go out for a few hours. Or if you wake up and your water is off.

It's your reminder that you have to be open minded and accept that things are done differently when you start thinking and saying we do it differently where I am from. It helps you learn to be ok when you start missing funerals, weddings, new births, naming ceremonies, graduations, summer cookouts and new Jordan releases. Your why will force you to use your imagination and turn that new Gregory Porter or Nas album into an imaginary concert because you won't be able to see them on tour. Your why renews your enthusiasm when you become exhausted.

> *"Enthusiasm is like a catalyst. When added to wisdom and experience you can produce small miracles. If you want to change hours into minutes, renew your enthusiasm."* - Author Unknown

Defining Your Personal Why

Your WHY will remind you that you can get through whatever temporary waiver in commitment you might be experiencing. Things will get rough. Your why will make you recall the promise you've made to yourself and your family that you will be successful in this move. It will serve as your argument or defense against those who disapprove of your move and try to talk you out of it. Your why will force you to look carefully at everything and make a very big decision about what's non-negotiable for you.

Beyond discovering why you want to move to Ghana it's also a good idea to review the things you like about being in America. Nine times out of 10, those things will not exist in Ghana, so arranging or rearranging your priorities is crucial. There are a lot of things we may take for granted in America because they are available to us without question. America far exceeds most places on the globe from an infrastructural perspective (roads, buildings, water, gas, electricity). It's the most powerful nation in the world and despite its challenges, more people from around the world would prefer to move to America than Americans would prefer to leave. Even with racism.

We know America's infrastructure was built on a few hundred years of free labor on the backs of kidnapped and enslaved Africans. With regard to infrastructure, Ghana is nearly a century behind the United States That's debatable but it's a worthy debate. So what does that mean to the daily life of the average person repatriating to Ghana? It means refilling your propane canisters or learning to cook outside over wood or coal – unless you follow a raw diet. It means limited underground state-provided water (depending on the area). It could mean sometimes not having running water from an indoor tap and keeping a bucket handy. It means shaky fiber optic telecommunications and internet reception more times than you'd like. It means bumpy and limited paved roads with horrible traffic and sometimes no traffic lights.

Defining Your Personal Why

It also means the opportunity to drill your own borehole (well) for access to fresh water hundreds of meters beneath the earth. It means the opportunity to install solar panels as a response to lack of electrical infrastructure. It means relaxing your body, adapting to the weather, and sweating out those hot Ghanaian nights once the sun goes down. Everywhere there is a perceived gap or deficit, there is also a real opportunity to live differently or work towards helping to create a change people may want and appreciate. But one thing is for sure, there is no American winter.

<<<<<<<Check out this article

It's one experience to visit and be shielded by the privilege of your blue passport and vacation budget to enjoy Ghana as a tourist. It's a different experience to live in Ghana. If you're going to make Ghana your home, your WHY needs to be bigger than where Ghanaian development, infrastructure and societal advancement are right now.

You may also want to ask yourself what development and infrastructure mean to you and if you're looking for Ghana "to be like America". Ask yourself if your idea of a developed neighborhood, society or nation is patterned after Western society. There is a lot to weigh, compare, review, and consider. Afterall, what good is the infrastructure if you get shot by cops for living and can't enjoy it?

Each of us is different. Our experiences and expectations are different. The breadth and depth of this conversation will not be the same for everyone. We live as differently in America across social, educational and economic strata as do Ghanaians. The distance between the haves and have nots is still a journey in Ghana. The difference is that you can leapfrog in Ghana by solving the right problem or seeing the right idea through. When money isn't a challenge, you may have it easier in some ways and more difficult in others.

Defining Your Personal Why

In my opinion, the challenges faced by single men will be less significant than those presented to women traveling and relocating alone or with children. But I also see benefits. While Ghana is a matriarchal society, there are cultural differences and deep history that deserve to explored and debated regarding women's rights. I'm careful not to apply and judge based on my American reality. Families and older relatives also have different factors to consider. Moving with children of any age also offers an additional level of complexity as there are different priorities when it comes to medical care, education, and mobility. You get the point. Everything matters!

At the same time, some of you may not feel like you need to explore your personal why as deeply as I am suggesting for a variety of reasons. You may be young enough to start all over. You may be financially secure enough to live at a certain level above pedestrian challenges. Some of you go hard in the paint like the Pistons in '88 and are willing to fight your way through. Some of you may have the "whatever is clever, we outchea" vibes. You may be a gut person or may feel yourself being pushed or called by a divine force. I believe every reason to explore your personal reasons why or why not are valid as long as you can be truthful with yourself, remain open minded, and manage yourself well.

For those of us who clearly want to breathe freely and connect with the continent in a very real everyday way by living, working, building, loving, fighting, learning, teaching, losing, winning and agree that at the end of your days you want to expire as a citizen or resident of Ghana (or whatever African country you choose) and leave a legacy for your future generations here - I maintain that this conversation of your personal why is tantamount to have with yourself and loved ones.

I've left the next few pages blank for you to begin to work and write out your why. If you want to re-read or reference something before you start writing, that's cool. I highly suggest you do this alone

Defining Your Personal Why

without any external noise - human or otherwise. If you have a spouse or other adult family members who are moving with you, I suggest they get their own book and/or work and write it out on their own before you begin to share and discuss with each other. Take your time and enjoy the process. FYI, I didn't go through this process before I moved but I am going through it now. Here are some simple prompts to help you get started.

Why are you moving? What will you need for yourself and your family? How adaptable are you to change? How do you respond when things do not go your way?

Scan and read this article before you start

The real question is do your write with a pen or a pencil?

Defining Your Personal Why

Defining Your Personal Why

WHY GHANA?

I don't feel that I am a visitor in Ghana or in any part of Africa. I feel that I am at home. I've been away for four hundred years, but not of my own volition, not of my own will. –**Omowale Malcolm X**

Why Ghana is a really BIG question and can be just as important for your planning process as discovering your personal why. Africa has 54 countries. It's dense. It's diverse. It's massive. In each country there are many ethnic groups. In each country there are many languages. Africa is the cradle of civilization. Africa is energy!

Outside of the nuances of each traditional culture you also have an intertwined mix of colonial culture and religion. You will find many countries carry characteristics of their colonizers - the most obvious being language and demeanor. If any proof or understanding is needed as to the impact of colonization, look at how many African countries have official languages that are not traditional or native.

From food, to mannerisms, to the justice system, the influence of colonizing nations on African countries remains strong and pervasive. In British and Dutch colonized nations, lawyers and judges still wear old school European wigs. French - breakfast is still coffee and French baguettes. Countries colonized by the British are very English and tea is commonplace. Although Italians never successfully colonized Ethiopia, every Ethiopian restaurant still serves spaghetti.

However, despite the pervasiveness of colonial culture and religion, proof of the bandwidth of our resilience is the fact that many African countries and their various ethnic groups have managed to keep a stronghold on elements of their traditions: language, art, food, symbolism, dress, spirituality, music, dance and more - separate from colonial influence. Ghana is a great

Why Ghana

example of this maintenance of culture. Having a deep appreciation, respect and understanding of how culture works will get you further than the dollar in a lot of instances.

There are so many choices and options in Africa although Ghana has been heavily featured in the news with regard to Diasporan "going home" and has maintained its prominence for Diasporan as the primary choice of landing.

Check out the ODANA Network>>>>>>

When I first came to Ghana in 2014, it was to gain a deeper spiritual discipline and learn more about manifesting through the traditional Akan way of life. My reasons for staying, building, living and wanting to help develop communities, although sparked by a spiritual foundation, are inherently selfish in that I believe I can live and be my best and most honest self here. Again, we will all have our individual journey, none better or more significant than the other.

In general, there are a number of historical and practical reasons for Black people to choose Ghana. Historically, Ghana has been very friendly and accepting of African Americans. It's rooted in Ghana's independence history most prominently through its first President Dr. Kwame Nkrumah credited with popularizing and developing the concepts of Pan Africanism.

Nkrumah deepened his early understanding of Pan Africanism as a student at Lincoln University - an historically Black college in Lincoln, PA. His study, writing, and exchanges with others during his time at Lincoln helped strengthen his foundation that would later help fuel Ghana's movement toward independence.

While at Lincoln, Dr. Nkrumah became a member of Phi Beta Sigma Fraternity, Incorporated – one of the 9 fraternities and sororities in the Pan Hellenic Council of Black fraternities and sororities. Osegeyfo – meaning redeemer – a name granted to

Why Ghana

Nkrumah by his compatriots – was also a student of the early civil rights movement and the teachings of Marcus Garvey. During his summers in the US, he spent time in Harlem listening to revolutionary street orators and studied the African American struggle. According to historian John Henrik Clarke, "the influence of the ten years that (Nkrumah) spent in the United States would have a lingering effect on the rest of his life." He also added:

> These evenings were a vital part of Kwame Nkrumah's American education. He was going to a university – the university of the Harlem Streets. This was no ordinary time and these street speakers were no ordinary men. The streets of Harlem were open forums, presided over [by] master speakers like Arthur Reed and his protege Ira Kemp. The young Carlos Cook, founder of the Garvey oriented African Pioneer Movement was on the scene, also bringing a nightly message to his street followers. Occasionally Suji Abdul Hamid, a champion of Harlem labour, held a night rally and demanded more jobs for blacks in their own community. This is part of the drama on the Harlem streets as the student Kwame Nkrumah walked and watched.

With the lessons he learned during Harlem summers in the streets, and his time in London turning theory into practice with George Padmore and the Pan African Congress, Nkrumah returned to Ghana with a perspective largely influenced by the struggles of Black Americans with civil rights and free speech in the U.S. If Nkrumah's Pan-African fervor was sparked in the U.S., it was refined in London.

<<<<<<<<More on Nkrumah

He returned to Ghana on fire and eventually was chosen as Prime Minister in 1952. He held that position until he was elected President of independent Ghana, the first independent African nation, the black shining star and gateway to Africa on March 6, 1957.

Why Ghana

Ghana's independence had an important impact on African American views of Africa. Because an African country had actually gained independence, Black Americans began to look to Ghana as the new "Promised Land". Ghana served as a symbol of inspiration for people of African descent. Africa was no longer just seen as a dark jungle ruled by Tarzan. It was now emerging as a place that gave Black people in America a new view of hope for themselves and Black people all over the world. Ghana served as an escape from the racism Black people experienced in the United States and the abuse they faced when they criticized the racism in America.

W. E. B. Dubois, Julian Bond, Maya Angelou, Malcolm X and Martin Luther King, Jr. are a few of the prominent African Americans who either visited or moved to Ghana beginning in the mid 1950's.

Nkrumah knew Ghana would need international connections to assist in its development and the independence of every other country on the African continent. He sought and welcomed African Americans into the country. Moreover, he brought American civil rights leaders into his inner circle as advisors and political allies. So, Ghana and its independence were crucial to African Americans and the growing Black liberation movement in the US.

Since the 1960's, Ghana has led the charge of African countries who have accepted African American repatriates. To this day, Ghana has the largest population of African Americans repatriates. More recently, Ghana has staunchly encouraged descendants of the victims of the Trans-Atlantic Slave Trade, to reconnect with the African continent.

Prior to the actual The Year of Return, under the leadership of its last two Presidents, Ghana has made several power moves towards "making Black people whole". The Right to Return is an idea that purports that Africans of the diaspora should have a right to return to Africa (not just Ghana) as victims of the Trans-Atlantic

Why Ghana

Slave Trade who were kidnapped and be made whole through citizenship. This idea was made popular by Diasporans who moved to Ghana.

More on Right of Abode>>>>>>>

In 2000, Ghana passed a law on the 'Right of Abode'. Not to be confused with citizenship, the Right of Abode allows a person of African descent to apply and be granted the right to stay in Ghana indefinitely. In December 2016 President John Mahama gifted citizenship to 34 Africans of the Diaspora living in Ghana based on the ideals of the Right to Return.

In his first presidential Term, H.E. Nana Addo Dankwa Akufo-Addo established the Office of Diaspora Affairs, Office of the President, which although originally set up to help bridge the gap between Ghanaians abroad and the country for the main purpose of investment, has now become much more actively involved as a key government stakeholder in the conversation with various diaspora groups fighting for a more streamlined and accessible avenue to citizenship.

<<<<<< During the Year of Return, the President gifted citizenship to 126 Diasporan Africans as a result of advocacy from various Diasporan groups in Ghana. I used the term gifted because in both instances, citizenship was the result of the will of the President. There is no direct, established pathway to citizenship in Ghana right now for Black people "returning home". However, The Year of Return and the energy around it have definitely sparked more conversations and energy around the possibility. So far, more than any other country, Ghana is showing promise as the Black Star of West Africa and making itself available to the diaspora. There is also currently a diaspora policy being developed and revised by the country of Ghana to

Why Ghana

include a dual definition of Diasporan - Ghanaians abroad and victims of the trans-Atlantic slave trade.

The Government of Ghana recently held a memorial service for George Floyd as a show of global solidarity to those protesting his wrongful death at the hands of police in Minneapolis, MN. During the program Ghana's then Minister of Tourism, the Honorable Barbara Oteng Gyasi, invited African Americans to come home to Ghana if they didn't feel comfortable or safe in the US.

There are several practical reasons Ghana is attractive to Black Americans who are choosing to repatriate:

1. Ghana is an English-speaking country. Although Ghana maintains its traditional languages – the most prevalent being Twi - English is the official language.

2. Ghana is easy to access by plane with a variety of relatively short and affordable flights on international carriers.

3. Ghana is a relatively safe country. Though crime is virtually inescapable, violent crimes – including shooting deaths – are not as frequent as in U.S.

4. Ghana has held peaceful democratic presidential elections for the past 20 years and is a relatively peaceful Nation.

5. Ghana has a great mix of tradition and modernity. Many modern amenities co-exist with the beauty of tradition and ancient cultural elements.

6. It's easy to access several other African countries via land or air. Ghana's Kotoka International Airport also offers regular flights to and from a number of European and Asian countries, as well. The airport was recently named the #1 airport in African.

7. The cost of living is relatively low compared to America and health care is accessible and affordable.

8. Ghana is the most developed Nation infrastructurally in West Africa and has been named one of the fastest developing Nations in West Africa.

9. Ghana offers a number of opportunities to make a deep and wide impact in industries where Black people have been traditionally locked out.

10. LOVE - More people than you may imagine have found love in Ghana. At least three people who have travelled with me over the years have gotten married.

Overall, Ghana has proven to be a welcoming "home" for Black people. The energy is off the charts. The weather is pretty much always amazing. The people are extremely welcoming. The enjoyment is endless. The food is amazing.

Ghana is not perfect by far. There are issues. Some small and some major. None that are insurmountable with unity, self-determination, cooperative economics, collective work and responsibility, purpose, creativity and faith. Your **Birthright** is awaiting your to claim in Ghana.

If there is no struggle, there is no progress. – Frederick Douglass

Take a Birthright Journey with The Adinkra Group>>>>>>>>>>>>>>

Why Ghana

Partner with us at TEAM CSR for Humanitarian projects

DEMOGRAPHICS: GHANA IS A COUNTRY

Demographics are important in general even in your home state but more important when you're considering moving to an unfamiliar place in a different zone and 5000 miles away from what you've known as home. Finding and defining home is important, and understanding the geographical and demographics play a part.

Geography

The Republic of Ghana is on the West coast of Africa with the Gulf of Guinea at its most southern border. It is bordered by Ivory Coast on the west, Burkina Faso on the north and Togo on the east. All three neighboring countries are accessible by air and land.

Ghana is about 87,854 sq. miles (227,500 Km²) with a population of approximately 31 million people. In comparison, it is approximately the size of Texas, Oregon or the UK but a bit smaller than California. This is important because people often talk about and reference Ghana in terms of Accra, its capital city, but not the whole country. For perspective, the United States is about 330 million people so Ghana is about 10% of the U.S. population. The percentage of Black people in the U.S. is about 14 percent of the population at about 40 Million. Which means there are just as many Black people in the whole United States as there are in Ghana. So, if living and existing in a sea of Blackness is important, Ghana be dey for you.

About 57% of the population in Ghana lives in cities (about 17,625,000 people in 2020) and the median age is about 22 with about 50/50 male/female gender split. Ghana, like most of the African continent, has a very youthful population. This is one of the

Demographics: Ghana is A Country

reasons Africa in general is so important to the world. Africa's population is expected to double by 2050.

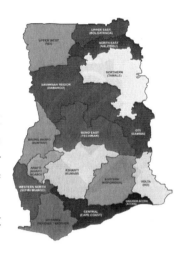

Ghana is organized into 16 regions - each with a capital city. As you can see with the majority of Ghana's population resting within its urban centers and a significant distance often coupled by bad roads to its most northern, eastern and western borders, it's easy to confuse or substitute Accra for Ghana. But if you're planning to move, be clear. Ghana is not Accra and Accra is not Ghana.

Most people who travel or move to Ghana seldom visit its less popular regions, but it's important to have an overall view of the landscape of the entire country.

One of the most important questions you should be asking yourself is where do I want to live in Ghana? People might always assume Accra or Kumasi since they're the most popular and could be seen as having the most developed infrastructure. They are also the most crowded and expensive. The same way you may be looking for a certain character in a neighborhood in the States, you should look for the same in Ghana. More importantly, how close you are to main thoroughfares, grocery stores, markets, malls, churches, mosques, entertainment venues, and other outlets makes a difference in your daily movement.

Ghana's Regions>>>>>>>>>>>>

Demographics: Ghana is A Country

Climate

Is it hot out there in Africa? The answer is simple – yes - #nomorewinters. Temperatures usually range between 21° and 32° Celsius - between 69 - 89 degrees Fahrenheit. Ghana uses the metric system (like most of the rest of the world) so it's a good idea to have an understanding of it, or a mobile app on hand for quick conversions. I don't think I've experienced 69 degrees in Ghana but I've definitely experienced 89 degrees and hotter. Ghana's 89 is not New York's 89. It's also useful to note that Ghana is the closest landmass to the center of the world (0 longitude and 0 latitude). There's something very special and magical about being close to the center of the world beyond the majority year round warm climate.

Ghana has two main seasons (weather patterns) annually that really offer different daily experiences depending on where in Ghana you live: the dry season and rainy season. Harmattan is a part of the dry season where the atmosphere is relatively dry as a result of the Northeast winds blowing from the Sahara Desert. This normally happens from the end of November to the middle of March.

In the Northern region, the rainy season lasts from approximately May to September. In the central region, along the coast, from April to October. And in the southern region, Accra, the rainy season can last from April to November with the heaviest rains coming May – July. However, in the Eastern region, the rainy season is shorter and goes from April to June, with a break in July and August, and a slight return in September and October. These statistics are standard for Ghana and don't take into account any change in weather pattern due to global warming or any other natural element that may alter Ghana's standard weather pattern.

Annual rainfall can vary from 600 mm to 2,200 mm (24 - 86 inches). Flooding is commonplace during the rainy reason. Depending on

Demographics: Ghana is A Country

where you have settled, streets can be closed off and flooded. Determining if your home will be susceptible to flooding is a question you want to ask and be sure about when you're either building or buying a home. Finding out and more importantly experiencing both the dry and rainy season where you plan to settle can also be important for you. As stated earlier, there's a different experience waiting for you depending on where you decide to call home in Ghana.

Let's be truthful and think about it for minute. How many people really care or watch the average or median annual rainfall unless they live in an area susceptible to flooding? Most of us really check the weather just so we know what to wear. I know some of you actually know this information for your hometown, region and the U.S. as well as an above average amount of basic/standard geographical facts, but I'd bet most don't. My point is most of us don't think about this in our everyday life.

For a lot of Black people (because there is nothing like Black summers), anything other than sunny days are an annoyance. But in Ghana, rain is a real live treasure in many places. It's a tool. It's water that's used for everyday living. It's treasured and collected. Rain means maybe somebody won't have to walk a mile or two twice a day carrying a bucket of water for the house.

In America, we pretty much experience all four seasons - Summer, Fall, Winter and Spring, and each of us has a good idea of what that looks like where we live. One thing for sure, I personally don't check the weather in Ghana. I dress more for my day than for the weather. However, if you are moving to Ghana because you want to flex your green thumb and invest or join the African agricultural revolution, this information and a much deeper breadth of knowledge is crucial for your crops.

Demographics: Ghana is A Country

Travel and Transportation

Ghana has one international airport, Kotoka International Airport that just recently as of December 2018 opened a new terminal with the ability to process over 1 million passengers per year. However, there are several other regional airports in the country. One in Takoradi – in the western region. Another in Tamale – in the northern region. And still another in Ho – the eastern region. These regional airports are extremely important if you're interested traversing Ghana more quickly. Kumasi airport in the Ashanti region is being developed to eventually become Ghana's second international airport.

Learn about Kotoka Airport >>>>>>>>>>>

Although only about 15% of the roads in Ghana are paved, the most common form of transportation are tro tro (public minibuses), taxis, and Okada (motorcycles). Each is their own unique experience. Ghana does not have a functioning passenger or freight railway as of the first quarter of 2021 but it's being negotiated. Ride sharing apps such as Uber and Bolt are available mainly in most urban areas.

Language

While English is the official language, Ghana has maintained the fluent use of its traditional languages. Twi is the most widely spoken language in Ghana. Other languages are Asante, Ewe, Fante, Boron (Brong), Dagomba, Dangme, Dagarte (Dagaba), Kokomba, Akyem and Ga. As you may expect, the ethnicities somewhat mirror the languages but many Ghanaians speak at least three traditional languages in addition to English. We'll talk more about the languages and ethnic groups later in the book as well.

Religion

Ghana is a majority Christian nation. The country ranks in the top three most churches per capita in the world. Its religious breakdown is about 72 percent Christian (Pentecostal, Protestant, and Catholic, mainly) 18 percent Muslim, and 5 percent traditional. It should be noted that while Ghana accepts almost all kinds of faith, you will find very aggressive and committed Christians who are unaccepting of any other faith. Interestingly enough, because traditional beliefs are so intertwined into daily culture, you'll find many traditional customs such as pouring libation and other forms of ancestor reverence still practiced and honored during traditional festivals and privately behind closed doors.

You will find many images of the blonde haired, blue eyed, white Jesus and people will be willing to fight you over them. Regardless of the religious preference you'll find many people in Ghana with a high level of reverence for spirituality and you'll see it in the names of their taxis, stores and busses. Jesus Walks Electronics or By His Grace Waakye. And although many may practice Christianity or Islam, there is a certain level of respect and reverence for traditional medicine, spirits, and rituals because they are powerful.

Wildlife and Ecotourism

Ghana is home to Lake Volta, the world's largest man-made lake, about 3,283 sq mi (8,500 sq km) which is located in the Volta Region. Lake Volta is also home to one of the the world's largest hydrodams - The Akosombo Dam, also known as the Volta Dam, built by Kwame Nkrumah. It's a beautiful site and if you have the opportunity to cruise and or stay on the lake, it's worth the drive from Accra. Ghana's highest point is Mount Afadjato which is 2900 ft. (885 M) also located in the Volta region.

The physical terrain in Ghana is composed primarily of low plains with several uplands and a major plateau in the south-central part

Demographics: Ghana is A Country

of the country. I am not going to go into too much more detail about the topographical landscape of Ghana but if you are an environmentalist, agriculturalist, or someone who loves the fresh air provided by nature, there are still many parts of Ghana you will enjoy and love.

I really think the legacy of Tarzan and how western media has portrayed Africa has caused the misconception that most of Africa is a Safari (yes the whole continent). Witnessing the animal kingdom live in the wild naturally is definitely exciting but all of Africa is not a Safari. The idea of an entire continent made of jungles and savanna land is an unfortunate stereotype. There are, however, many places in Ghana to witness wildlife living in their natural habitat where you can take day trips or even spend several nights.

The Mole National Park is about 736 km^2 in the western part of the northern region of Damonoyo. This nature preserve is home to elephants, hippos, and several species of birds including eagles, kites and hornbills. The Digya National Park on the shores of Lake Volta has hippos, water bucks, crocodiles and manatees. Safari Valley is Ghana's newest addition to its growing Ecotourism. It's an absolutely breathtaking and amazing high-end ecotourism vacation resort committed to growing it's wild animal population.

Follow Safari Valley on Instagram >>>>>

Economics

I think most of us know the economic foundation of the United States of America was based on the labor of enslaved kidnapped Africans throughout America's developmental eras to current day. The strength and power of a nation is determined by its gross domestic product (GDP). The GDP of a nation at its basic definition is an estimate of the total value of all the goods and services it

Demographics: Ghana is A Country

produced during a specific period. The Military (which I wouldn't define as power as much as I would as a result of power) is supported by the GDP and amount of expendable resources a nation has to spend or trade which supports its investment in its military.

For perspective, The US GDP is 20 trillion (the highest on the globe). Ghana's GDP is 65 billion for Ghana. The top 7 largest state budgets in the U.S. each has a budget larger than the GDP of Ghana. Knowing these figures will provide you with a basic understanding of how the GDP, exports and imports have a direct effect on you during your repatriation Journey.

Imports and Exports

The more a country can grow, produce or develop on its own - or maintain fair trade relations with a country who can provide these products, the less expensive those items are in the country. The more a nation can develop those industries to export local products and raw resources, or invest in its human capital to innovate its industries and produce the products it needs for its nation's survival or that other Nations need and can be leveraged for trade, the more power a Nation has earned.

As a resident or citizen of Ghana who will rely on indigenous and foreign imported brands and products, you will want to find high quality products and food items at reasonable prices and availability. This is the direct connection or correlation to Ghana's GDP, import and export industries to your repatriation.

It's important that I speak to potential business owners and investors with regard to understanding the perspective I am presenting. Production and manufacturing are where you will find many of the long term opportunities to build generational wealth. You can help to develop an industry by creating a measurable product or service that has a measurable and meaningful effect on

Demographics: Ghana is A Country

the GDP a lot easier in Ghana. I have a saying that you don't move to Africa to get a job, you move to Africa to create jobs. It is much easier to see your role in the value chain of a country with a GDP of $65 billion as opposed to 20 trillion. Participating in a smaller economy means your contribution has a much greater, and more noticeable impact.

Follow Ghana's Economy>>>>>>>>>

Ghana's top exports are gold, crude petroleum, cocoa beans, cocoa paste, coconuts, brazil nuts, and cashews. The top imports of Ghana are refined petroleum, cars, rice, non-fillet frozen fish and delivery trucks. Ghana exports mostly to India, Switzerland, China, South Africa and United Arab Emirates; and imports mostly from China, United States, Netherlands, India and United Kingdom.

Ghana, its people, land, resources, and cultures are varied. If you're repatriating, take the time to learn as much as you can about the whole country. It's not only beneficial to you but's also a matter of respect. We must remember that America as a nation, while dominant, is an infant amongst elders in the world of nations.

Come with the intent to learn as much as possible and move in alignment with the country. Repatriating to Ghana or any African country for people of African descent, is special. Your ancestral memory is alive and working its way back through your DNA to all your senses so home will find you.

Demographics: Ghana is A Country

Check out Kustom Looks Clothier

KNOW SOME HISTORY (SMALL SMALL)

History is not everything, but it is a starting point. History is a clock that people use to tell their political and cultural time of day. It is a compass they use to find themselves on the map of human geography. It tells them where they are but, more importantly, what they must be. - Dr. John Henrick Clarke

Having a basic understanding of the history of a country you intend to visit is important. Also understanding that the history of Ghana – like the history of any other country – is something that is not static. It is a constantly evolving, developing phenomenon. History is neither interpreted nor applied consistently by anyone. Your job is learning and intentionally aligning history with who you are and how you choose to exist. For African descendants who are repatriating, learning and understanding the history can't and shouldn't be arbitrary.

African Americans often have an over-emotional attachment and romantic perspective of and being in Africa. We have a longing to be home and love our people because of our ancestral memory and the cosmic alignment that lies in our DNA. So when we visit and/or move, we want to believe that we are home automatically. And that home has been waiting for us to return. That everyone is waiting to welcome us with open arms and help us adjust. We forget or ignore that in our intentional separation over the past 600 years, a lot has changed. That the trans-Atlantic slave trade and its lingering policies separated us from our homeland and changed the nature of our relationship with our motherland and our people.

And no matter how much we want to be pure 100% African, the reality is that we all have adopted various characteristics of our colonizers. As much as we love the idea of being "home" and connecting with the continent, we have to understand that there is a disconnect that requires some work to reconnect. A big part of reconnecting is studying and learning the history of Africa and

Know Some History (Small Small)

Ghana, from a clean and fair African lens – as well as teaching and sharing African American history with those you meet.

Learning the history of Ghana will assist you in better shaping your overall worldview in understanding some of what you will encounter and experience as you begin to integrate into Ghanaian society. Learning History will also contribute to your recognition of various ethnic groups, their traditions, culture and characteristics; and assist as you move through and between socio-economic groups and begin allowing parts of Ghana to become a part of you.

History of Ghana in 10 minutes>>>>>>>>

Having at least a comprehensive overview understanding of the history of Ghana and its myriad cultures will serve as an invaluable social currency. Ghanaians are an extremely proud people. They are very family oriented. Their lineages, names and families are very much intertwined with their pride and often seem as old as time itself. As you begin to build relationships with people who you will call friends and family and show an authentic interest and connection to Ghanaian history, these newfound friends and family will begin to open doors and invite you into a deeper Ghanaian way of life that most tourists only experience from its outer most shell.

We all operate with a different understanding of the importance of history and it's modern day application and relevance towards the future. It's more important to some than others. If you don't know much about Ghana, its history or culture we will provide a foundational level from which you can grow your knowledge and understanding. There are tons of well-written books and articles that discuss Ghanaian history and culture from an African centered perspective and not through the eyes of colonizers.

Know Some History (Small Small)

Ghana and its people like most African nations have a long rich history that deserves exploration. The United States of America as a country and corporate body was founded in 1776, making the country only 244 years old as of 2020. Ghana is much older than its name, independence date, and geographical borders.

Most of us have been raised and taught American history in school devoid of Black contributions with an historically inaccurate focus on the history of Black people as enslaved / kidnapped people without any focus on the history or lives of Black people before enslavement throughout primary and secondary school. Most of our foundational understanding of history is rooted and viewed through our interaction with European history. Many of us who have decided to research and discover the truth about who we are did so in college and/or were lucky enough to have parents, teachers or mentors who pushed us towards seeking the truth about Black/African people and history. Our relationship with our oppressor is fairly new and still fresh. We still feel the sting of the whip through choke holds and bullets. While there are those of us ready to fully forgive and integrate our spirits, many of us are waking up.

What you may find in Ghana that is underscored by history is often a very different relationship with the colonizer and their culture - one that seems to be filled with love, admiration, and affection. You will begin to see how much African people love white people and do their best to emulate them - Stockholm syndrome. Stockholm syndrome is a psychological response. It occurs when hostages or abuse victims bond with their captors or abusers. This psychological connection develops over the course of the days, weeks, months, or even years of captivity or abuse. And in our case the abuse has been for generations.

Understanding the history, breadth, depth and variety of European invasion and inculturation in Ghana will assist you in understanding this without judgment. It will help you understand the intense reverent attitudes towards non-African people and all things foreign. It can feel disappointing and glaring because it's not supposed to be this way in Africa, right? You're in the mother land and the sun is glistening on your whipped shea butter covered body. This can be very disappointing for many of us returning to our "homeland" with a polar opposite relationship with our terrorizer.

What's more interesting is that their colonizer and our terrorizer are the same people. We have the same obstacle in many ways but our relationship with them is different based on which side of the colonization coin we fall - the families who stayed and were able to maintain what they could versus the families who were kidnapped and brought to America where we established a new family lineage and culture for ourselves.

This chapter will not go into fine detail or provide a succinct timeline about Ghana's history. Instead, I've invited a brother and friend who I know is passionate about history and Ghana. He is well read and uses his life force for the benefit of African people. I am grateful to him for lending his voice, perspective, and scholarship.

Introducing Gbontwi Anyetei>>>>>>>>>

Introduction

With art and national languages given pride of place around Ghana, upon arrival it can look like Ghana is a fully functioning state with all her philosophies and collective esteem intact and healthy. This is false though, and furthermore Ghana about which we have not been spared from miseducation. These are omissions

Know Some History (Small Small)

and lies in history that would instil pride, prevent repeat of mistakes, and ensure better placed loyalties and philosophies.

Everywhere you go in Ghana there are incidents or in dusty sleeves in our limited libraries there are references only remembered or known by a few. These few are unable to tell the story with the volume or regularity that Europeans tell the stories they've built their own version of civilisation on. A version they impose on the whole world daily, a version Africa is especially vulnerable whilst our history is erased or distorted.

Do not underestimate the change made by the traumas discussed above and most tragically do not underestimate how much has been forgotten. Even more frustrating is the pride holders of spiritual systems and traditional governance systems take in not passing along the most esoteric intelligence and values. 'A tsoo moko shishi' is a Ga saying which literally translates into 'We don't show the bottom' or 'meaning'. This is especially sad in the face of how death of mantses ('land fathers' or 'king' for want of a better word) and wulomei (traditional priests) not only cuts off possible learning but the lack of precautions taken to protect us against losses is fatal and irreversible. This lack of protection is present in every other field of African life so aggregates the ongoing damage.

Changing this and finding a way to record or archive what we're losing to death and cultural and economic vultures. This means the visitor to Ghana should be ideally well studied and share what they know about what we the residents have sometimes forgotten. Also ideal from either side is forgiveness or empathy for the hurtful things said out of ignorance. Miseducation merely looks different depending on where in the world you're coming from.

In academic and Pan-Africanist circles a lot is made of the coming of Arabs and Europeans and how colonisation stunted our progress and left our natural development arrested . This is undisputable. What also happened though is that Ghanaian traditions and culture that we think were somehow enshrined by some special set of circumstances have been just as manipulated and co-opted for foreign interests.

Corporal punishment, sexuality, polygamy, subjugation of women, gender roles are thought of as pillars of African 'culture'. But there's evidence presented by historians and scholars like France Cress Welsing, Marimba Ani and Ivan Sertima that many maladaptive parts of what we call culture are creations of colonists.

So we have the foreign inflicted damage and 'progress' we acknowledge, mourn and even seek to redress if possible and then we have these hidden corruptions that we think belong to Ga, Ewe, Asante, Ghanaian or African. Whilst we seek, scrutinise and identify solutions to the former we protect the latter along with problematic behaviours that follow along from these. Very often behaviours that were actually imposed to hurt and exploit our societies are even misconstrued to have helped us survive colonial pain.

Interchangeable Ethnic Conflict & Cooperation

The Ga were allied with the Asante in many conflicts before 1824. In 1824 the Ga allied with the Fante in a battle against the Asante in what is today called the Central region of Ghana.

The Akwamu and Ga were in pitched battles going back to the 1600s. Then in the late 1800s a Ga man established cocoa farms in lands adjacent to Akwamu territory in an area called Mampong.

Walter Rodney writes in his book How Europe Underdeveloped Africa "members of a 'tribe were seldom all members of the same political unit and very seldom indeed did they all share a common social purpose in terms of activities such as trade and warfare. Instead, African states were sometimes based entirely on part of the members of a given ethnic group or (more usually) on an amalgamation of members of different ethnic communities. All of the large states of 19th-century Africa were multiethnic, and their expansion was continually making anything like 'tribal' loyalty a thing of the past, by substituting in its place national and class ties..."

These realities I've just described once again speak to several things:

1. There is multiplicity to our experiences and identities. This multiplicity was okay in the past as it is today.

2. Battles and wars took place as they did across the world and those wars would have come to natural conclusions often transitioning to alliances or other forms of peace. There was nothing especially savage about or inevitable about 'tribal wars'. But these fights were entrenched by European alliances with their weaponised gunpowder, the trade in the enslaved, and colonisation. Western Europeans took divide and conquer tactics from the Romans and perfected them on south Saharan countries.

3. There has always been as much cooperation between African peoples as there has been conflict. This history is no different in Ghana but we have been unable to accept or even celebrate that about ourselves. Self-hate leads us to propagating falsehoods of only slaughtering ourselves in never-ending wars with liberal use of satanic religions.

Migration

In Yosef Ben Jochannan's book 'The Black Man of the Nile' he describes the existence and the condition of the Black Africans that inhabited ancient lands and Chancellor Williams' 'The Destruction of Black Civilisation' relates the mechanics of how these societies were broken up and refugees set out looking for the countries we today find ourselves from.

Know Some History (Small Small)

Related to the subject of ethnic relationships, is the question of migration. Especially how arrivals and departures of people impacted the cooperation and conflict referenced above. The migration of Ghana's peoples is a very common theme in education, stories and Ghanaian arts but not something consciously articulated. For example, the Hausa people in the north are common across most West African states. They are not only in Ghana but Ivory Coast, Togo, Benin and Nigeria, where they are the majority and hold some political power. They and many other northern people embrace their legacy of journey makers. The southern tribes claim an ancient indigenous status whilst contradicting stories are told elsewhere of their founding.

Ghana came by its name because the majority of the current population are from what is today called Mali. An old empire stood there either called Ghana or (had a significant king named Ghana). Historians are yet to agree. The Akan people that were brought to Ghana are the Asante, Fante and Nzima who hailed from there whilst those of Gadangme hailed from the east, i.e. Nile delta area.

Looking at the people and placements in Africa south of the Sahara affords us the opportunity to look at:

- How the establishment or lack thereof of nations impacted the chattel slave trade and colonisation.

- The psychology including shared vision, solidarity and trust that must have existed between people choosing to travel and live together and whether it's still present

- The traumas that were or weren't left behind in source countries

- The pre-capitalist commerce, priorities and technology that had our ancestors choose what is today called Accra, Takoradi and Tamale

- What we picked up and left behind along the way

Know Some History (Small Small)

European Atrocities

The British, the Dutch, the Danish, the Portuguese and the Germans waged many military campaigns against the people of the area today called Ghana. These armies and navies inflicted much damage that we haven't properly recorded. For us to fully comprehend Africa's physical damage from colonialism and infrastructure damage we have to try to begin calculating what mental and emotional trauma accompanied the fires and ballistics it took to wipe away structures and our memories of them.

An essential book I will recommend here is one called 'African Towns and Cities Before European Conquest' by Sir Richard Hull. This book singularly destroys every illusion most Africans and non-Africans have about the lack of whatever we call 'development' or 'civilisation' before white people. Beyond castles, there were mining efforts, grain store silos, multi-storey structures and design ideals we still haven't regained. When we factor in the cultural unity of Black Africa (there's also a book with that title by Cheikh Anta Diop), we are able to believe that even where there are no remains like the iron smelting works of the Nok in modern Nigeria or castle walls like those of great Zimbabwe –there were structures like those across Africa that colonisers eliminated completely.

 A visitor to Ghana will mostly see architecture styles in favour of European styles and even the non-built spaces like compounds are reducing or losing their community functions and reverence of nature. Even most of the existing road networks in Ghana, as in former colonies were designed for extraction of resources to enrich foreign antagonists.

These deteriorating and maladaptive changes in our environments and the way Africans think are all results of these attacks. Seeking accurate history and the words of Dutch visitors said of Benin, "These people are in no way inferior to the Dutch" (captured by

Know Some History (Small Small)

Walter Rodney again). African stories are necessary for regaining what we've lost. This journey has begun but has to be sustained.

European attacks took different forms. Foot troops of course with documented terrorisation, rapes and massive looting in the aftermath; bombardments from coastal castles; and the repatriation of art and other treasures is a conversation only now being approached meaningfully. In 1854 the British brought one of the biggest warships in their fleet called the HMS Scourge to destroy four of Accra's seven towns. This was a genocide of the Ga people who founded Accra and still survive although their language and population are now outnumbered in Ghana. The three times the British set fire to Kumasi were organised blazes.

Acknowledgement of these traumas is rare, even elusive and the healing that must follow can't happen before acknowledgement is commonplace. In the meantime we can appreciate how and why there was resistance by Ghanaians because it's only natural with our lives and freedoms being constantly ended.

Resistance and Contradictions

There's an African saying that 'When you fall you should look at where you tripped and not where you landed.' The world looks at where Africa has landed. Most harmfully, Africans in particular not only zoom in on our fallen position exclusively but we too often forget the falling part and act like this place of imbalance and ignominy in mud globally is our permanent and rightful place. A lie that in this case shapes Ghanaians' low self-esteem and many neuroses.

Franz Fanon wrote that it takes "a metaphysical experience" to understand racism. I respectfully disagree although it might be a semantic point. Ghanaians like all Africans 'understand' racism and the sheer unfairness of Europe and Europeans being the haves and Africa and Africans being the have-nots although we're holders of all the resources. Possibly encoded into the trauma we all carry around is some genetic memory of the bombardments, genocides and looting.

The difference is in the way the system of white supremacy warped history is depicted. No era passed of the Atlantic chattel slavery period in which there wasn't resistance from patriotic or simply prideful leaders. But we are left with a vacuum of truth about how we fought which would help us hold onto our humanity and the redemption there-in. This should mean that the descendants of these people should have a very clear idea of the danger Europeans have represented and some kind of memory of the way we've always resisted. Alas, this is not the case.

Unfortunately, as mentioned before history has been one of the victims of neoliberal priorities. Even the heroes we do have are depicted in sanitised ways and hardly retain pride that instills a sense of power.

For instance, I attended a play late in 2019 that reduced Yaa Asantewaa's rebellion as being motivated by wanting to retain the Asante stool. The nationalism at play in her acts, what it meant about the way women's voices were heard up to the nineteenth century. and her clarity of vision about the danger the 'English gentlemen' represented, are all left out of the play. It was only a shiny stool with nebulous spiritual importance that concerned the great Yaa Asantewaa which does her, the Asante, and Ghana a disservice. Nationhood was very much paramount for Yaa Asantewaa and we should never let ourselves forget this. When the Asante spent the 1800s fighting Europe it was about nationhood.

When members of the Ga resisted the English in 1854, the Danes and the Portuguese before them it was about nationhood. When Badu of the Fante wouldn't stop fighting until the Dutch chopped his head off and sent it to Holland it was about nationhood. The

British took firstborn sons of notable northern people in order to compromise what they would come to believe about nationhood. When John Mensah Sarbah and at least four Cape Coast lawyers took the British crown to court in Britain in order to establish the illegality of colonial rule it was to make sure British sovereignty in the Gold Coast was challenged, publicly intelligently and in a forum the British citizen respected and couldn't challenge.

Nkrumah in America

Kwame Nkrumah's time in America and how it impacted his return to Ghana (then Gold Coast) has been written about extensively. There are many essays and chapters in books like this one discussing the role of European or American travel on the minds and hearts of many an African independence leader.

There's much potential and cause for hope, lessons plus calls to action for us in studying the Nkrumah that returned from America but there's also the neglected side which is the Nkrumah before he travelled. It carries so much learning for us about the colonised subject and what we think we know about resistance for Africans south of the Sahara before the successful independence action of the fifties and sixties. There are a lot of interesting signposts in Nkrumah's life 1909 to 1936 (the latter being the year he left for the state of Pennsylvania in eastern United States) that start to tell that tale if we follow them

I have written a movie screenplay biopic about Kwame Nkrumah. The wealth of undeveloped understanding is one of the reasons that I chose Nkrumah's life before independence as the focus of the film. His presidency hasn't been celebrated enough in my opinion but he's at least known of in every country I have travelled to. His dramatic foreign-sponsored removal from power in Africa's troubled 60s are also covered frequently. His younger years are outright neglected though and much in need of learning from.

Know Some History (Small Small)

Let's start from what is as good a beginning as any. Nkrumah's trip to America didn't birth Nkrumah's revolutionary spirit. This misunderstanding is a lost opportunity to appreciate the nuance of the continental African vocabulary of resistance. This closes a door people might walk through to follow-up like the court case of Fante and the work of Kwegyir Aggrey who educated Nkrumah at the Achimota School (then known as the Prince of Wales College).

In America, Africa, Europe or wherever political expression amongst the African Diaspora was suppressed. In colonised Africa even many cultural events were not allowed unless a white man was present or being celebrated.

In colonised Africa, documents like Garvey's World were banned. This is hard to revisit in this neo-liberal world where information and internet appears free uncensored and 'knowledge' encouraged.

In a Black Lives Matter world outspoken words and actions popular and rightly so. Most importantly, iconic moments created have been effective. Some understanding of the world where all expression and suppressed could better help study in approaching corridors where a just light is yet to shine.

Nkrumah's visionary engagement with women was unfortunately unique —even amongst Africa's socialist independent leaders and especially in the world in general. The source of this may have been his mother, the third of Nkrumah's father's wives. It may have been his rural upbringing where a proper and healthy status of Women had not been as directly attacked by colonists with their agents to change value systems. Walter Rodney again said "some women had real power in the political sense, exercised either through religion or directly within the politico-constitutional apparatus" or did it come from Nkrumah's strong Black women from within the revolutionaries he met in 1940's America or 1950s Gold Coast —girlfriends or comrades.

Know Some History (Small Small)

Wealthy market women were major funders of Kwame Nkrumah's anti-colonial action and running of his CPP (Convention People's Party) so we can even argue that prominently positioned women was simply logical politics. That's if we're putting idealism to the side.

The Civil Rights movement all the way up until the seventies had challenges in how it dealt with women. To make sure he and the nation that was about to become Ghana didn't make these same mistakes may all have been part of Nkrumah's intentionality.

The designer of Ghana's flag was a woman —Theodosia Okoh. Mabel Dove known as Ghana's first radical feminist and also a poet wrote in Nkrumah's newspaper —Accra Evening News and it's replacement Ghana Evening News. She later became one of Nkrumah's record making number of ministers in his parliament These women don't have the prominence this writer would like and the gains in women's political presence were mostly reversed by the military and puppet regimes enforced on Ghana by the coups after Nkrumah.

What America undoubtedly did and life in historically Black colleges and universities of all places was awakening future leaders to be unapologetic and convinced of their genius and the fallibility of whiteness.

Safe Spaces

The networks it takes to start building and refining in order to maximise learning for every individual can take months of being on the ground in Ghana. It's then that you guarantee yourself access to the WhatsApp groups and Instagram statuses where you're a recognised participant in the thread.

- **University of Legon** – especially the 'Institute of African Studies'. Pre-covid, seminars and film screenings were taking

Know Some History (Small Small)

place here on a regular basis which guarantees progressive, pan-Africanist and innovative discourse.

- **Terra Alta** – hosts plays and discussion nights on neglected subjects like gender based violence, sexuality and the environment.

- **Ahaspora** – is a professional networking email list-serve group which should be joined as soon as possible. Information about events and securing creature comforts.

- **Freedom Centre, Kokomlemle.** The most public facing pan-Africanist Centre. When Cuban, Venezuelan or formerly Libyan ambassadors want a listening ear among Africans not indebted to international white monetary capital they come and speak at the Freedom Centre. The Freedom Centre also operates the Insight newspaper.

- **Abibitumi** is an app founded by a naturalised Ghanaian citizen (and professor at Legon University, IAS) where intense pan-Africanist conversations take place

- **WEB Du Bois Centre, Cantonments.** The building that was the home of great African-American leader is now a museum and the compound a hub of Diaspora diplomacy in Ghana.

Bibliography:

'*The Destruction of Black Civilization*' – Chancellor Williams
'*How Europe Underdeveloped Africa*' –Walter Rodney
'*Towards Colonial Freedom*' – Franz Fanon
'*The Black Man of the Nile*' – Yosef Ben Jochannon
'*Capitalism and Slavery*' – Eric Williams
'*The History of the Gold Coast and the Asante*' – Christian Reindorf
'*African Towns And Cities Before European Conquest*' - Richard Hull

Know Some History (Small Small)

Check out Spinal Clinic Ltd in Ghana

ALL BLACK PEOPLE LOOK ALIKE: ETHNICITY AND LANGUAGE

All Black people don't look alike but all Black people do have a doppelgänger somewhere in Africa. Growing up with Diallo as my first name made a great way to meet and get to know brothers and sisters from the continent and a great way for them to meet me.

Native west Africans often assumed I was from Senegal because Diallo is a common family name from the Fulani, and they were sometimes disappointed when I said Trenton. And in Trenton I grew up on a block with two Diallo's: Baba Diallo and Big Diallo. I'm still little Diallo.

And every West African country I've travelled in, I was assumed to be from wherever I was until I spoke. Some refused and just said, "whatever, you're African", because they couldn't figure out where in Africa Trenton is. And others debated me on if I was African or American. Many of my Senegalese family refuse to call me Diallo as my first name so I am Sumbry Diallo to them to this day.

Historically and culturally, we are not African. We migrated to become Yoruba, Mende, Temne, Wolof, Zulu, Mandika, Susu, Akan, Ewe, Fante, Ebo, Fulani, Ateke, etc. Identity to this unique cultural group was one of the things we lost in our kidnapping. Our resilience has proven itself. We've been able to maintain much of our cultural and ancestral memory in how we operate now. Our ability to recreate new cultural norms for ourselves is evident throughout the United States. Black is just not a deep or wide enough expression to encompass our collective composition but it's really all we have.

Prior to the political division of Africa by Europeans who during the 1884 Berlin Conference, most of Africa was organized and regulated by ethnicity. Ghana was no different. To this day, you will

All Black People Look Alike: Ethnicity & Language

find some separation by ethnic groups based on the history of where people settled but intermixing is unavoidable.

Ghana's main modern day ethnic groups are the Akan, Ewe, Ga, and Fante. The ethnic groups and languages are directly intertwined although you'll often find slight differences to the way the same language is spoken in various parts of Ghana based on geographical location.

Outside of not being an ignorant American, understanding there are different ethnic groups with unique history between them outside of the overall Ghanaian history with the European, will help you understand much of what you may encounter often known as tribalism and most importantly, help you stay out of it. Each ethnic group has its own different cultural practices, protocols and language variations. The same way codes and keys to surviving in Black American cities are integral to the culture and language of our "ethnic groups", Ghana is the same. In DC, "Bamma", "Joe", or "Moe" have multiple meanings. If you say, "what up doe?", we know you're from Detroit. While we don't have technical African American ethnic groups, we have noticeably different cultural norms often based on where in the United States we settled. Our geographical location has helped us define our "Black American ethnicity". Each of our cultural norms are accompanied by our own spoken form of English.

My next guest contributor has a vast and profound breadth of knowledge and perspective on Black people. I am beyond thrilled that he has agreed to participate and lend his voice to the subject of Ethnicity and Languages.

Introducing Ọbádélé Bakari Kambon, Ph.D>>>

All Black People Look Alike: Ethnicity & Language

Of Repatriation, Rivers and Rivulets

1. ḥʿ.k	stand.2SG
	'You stand'
	ḏd mdw
	speak word.PL
	'words spoken'
	ẖnti
	front
	'in front of'
	kmtyw
	Black.HUM.PL
	Black people
	ḥpw
	Hpw
	'Apis bull'
	.is
	like

The fact is we are Black. In fact, the first instance of us referring to ourselves as such dates back to bɛyɛ sɛ 2289-2255 BCE in the Pyramid text of Pepi (I) MeryRa:[i] The vertical text to the left in example (1) states "You stand in front of the Black people like the Apis bull". The Apis bull was a Black bull. Interestingly, in the exact same period, again under nswt bity mry-ra sA Ra pipi 'Nswt Bity Mery-Ra Sa Ra Pepi' we also find individuals referring to themselves as Black as evidenced in example (2):

a.   a.

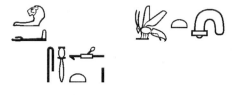

Ḥȝty-ʿ   ḫtm(ty) bity   smr wʿty

Mayor   sealer Lower   Kemet ruler.POSS   sole companion

 ẖry-ḥbt

carrier-ritual book

'Mayor, seal-bearer of the Ruler of Lower Kemet, unique companion, carrier of ritual book'

imy-r ḥm(w)-nṯr

PREP-mouth servant(s) Netcher

'overseer of the servant(s) of the Netcher'

imy-r šmʿ mȝʿ   Ppy-n-ʿnḫ

within-mouth Upper Kmt true Pepi-POSS-life

rn.f nfr

name.3M.SG good

'The true overseer of Upper Kemet, Ni-ankh-Pepi, his good name'

Ḥpi km

Hepi Black

'Black Hepi'

    b.

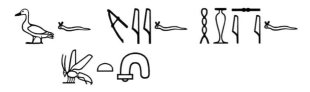

sȝ.f   mry.f   ḥsy.f   ḫtm(ty) bity

son.3M.SG   beloved.3M.SG praised.3M.SG sealer Lower Kmt

'His son, his beloved, his praised, the seal-bearer of the ruler of Lower Kemet'

smr wʻty   imy-r ḥm nṯr   ppy ʻnḫ   rn.f nfr

companion sole PREP-mouth servant Neṯer Pepi-life name.3M.SG good

'Unique companion, overseer of the servants of the netcher; Pepi-ankh, his good name'

Ḥny(t)   km

Henenit   Black

'**Black** Henenit'[ii]

Figure 1: Depiction of imAxw Henenit Km (Black Henenit) making an incense offering to imAxw Hepi Km (Black Hepi)

And how do we know that ⌀ km translated to Black? The same word has been preserved lexically (with regard to form) and semantically (with regard to meaning) in Coptic—the last phase of the written language, which continues to be spoken as a liturgical language as demonstrated below in the following excerpt from the Song of Solomon, which reads:

b. [ⲁⲛⲟⲕ ⲁⲛⲅ   ⲟ]ⲅⲕⲁⲙⲏ   ⲁλλⲁ   ⲛⲉⲥⲱⲉⲓ
   anok ang   ou.kamē   alla   nesōei

   1SG   1SG   INDF ART.**Black**   but   beautiful

'I am **Black** but beautiful'

[…]

[ⲙⲡⲣ 6]ⲱⲱ☐ ⲉⲣⲟ ⲉⲓ   ⲭⲉ   ⲁⲛ☐
ⲟⲅⲕⲁⲙⲏ   [ⲁⲛ]ⲟⲕ.

mpr   chōsht   ero ei   de   ang
ou.kamē   anok

NEG   look   PREP 1SG   because   1SG
INDF ART.**Black**   1SG

'[Don't] look at me because I'm **Black**'[iii]

In fact, in various languages of the continent now known as Afrika, from classical to contemporary times, we find a similar conception of individual and extended self as demonstrated in the table below:

Table 1: Afrika and Afrikan in Contemporary Afrikan Languages

1. Akan (Ghana)
a. O-bibi-ni[iv]

   NOM.HUM-Black-NOM.HUM

   'Afrikan (lit. Black person)'

b. A-bibi-man

2. Yorùbá (Nigeria)
a. A-dú-ɼ-àwọ̀

   NOM.HUM-Black-in-color

   'Afrikan (lit. Black person)'

b. Ilẹ̀   A-dú-ɼ-àwọ̀

All Black People Look Alike: Ethnicity & Language

NOM-Black-nation/land

'Afrika (lit. Nation/Land of Blacks)'

land NOM.HUM-Black-in-color

'Afrika (lit. Land of Blacks)'

3. **Bambara (Mali)**
a. Fara-fin

human-Black

'Afrikan (lit. Black person)'

b. Fara-fin-na

human-Black-LOC

'Land of the Black people (Afrika)'[v]

4. **Wolof (Senegal)**
a. Nit ku ñuul

human GEN Black

'Afrikan (lit. Black person)'

b. Réewu nit ku ñuul

land human GEN Black

'Afrika'

5. **Kikôngo (Congo DRC)**
a. N'dômbe

HUM.Black

« Noir, Noire » 'Black male, Black female'[vi]

b. Nsi ya Bandômbe

land GEN Black.PL

'Afrika (lit. land of Black people)'

6. **Igbo (Nigeria)**
c. Ndi isi ojii

HUM head Black

'Afrikans (lit. Black people)'[vii]

d. Ala ndi isi ojii

land people head Black

Afrika (lit. land of Black people)[viii]

All Black People Look Alike: Ethnicity & Language

Again, while it may be assumed that these are relatively recent coinages and/or calques, in reality, we can trace this terminological self-identification as Black all the way back to ancient ⌂𓃭⊗ Kmt 'The Black Nation/Land of the Blacks' mentioned above and as shown in the following examples:

7. 𓎛 Mdw Ntr 'Hieroglyphs'

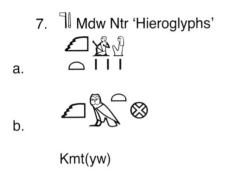

a.

b.

    Kmt(yw)   Kmt

    'Black People' [ix,x,xi]   'The Black Nation/Land of the Blacks'[xii]

While for years, primarily white Egyptologists and a few of their phenotypically-Black-on-the-outside-but-anti-Black-on-the-inside lackeys have claimed that the term ⌂𓃭⊗ Kmt 'The Black Nation/Land of the Blacks' refers to cultivable Black soil, they seem to have failed to take into account that the ⌂𓃭 Kmt(yw) 'Black People' themselves, in their mythology, said that they were made by 𓎸𓃭𓏏𓅱 Ḫnmw 'Khnum' on his potter's wheel out of that exact same soil. This means that if the soil is Black, so too are the people made from that soil. Check and mate. Evidence in support of this fact can be seen, for example, in the temple to 𓎸𓃭𓏏𓅱 Ḫnmw 'Khnum' at Esna where it states:

8.

    nḥp.sn   ṯrw   ḥr   nḥp.f

form.3PL ochre (from 3bw island) on potter's wheel.3M.SG

'Formed them of ochre (from Abw island) on his potter's wheel.'[xiii]

Interestingly, 𓉢𓃘𓃀𓏲𓈅 3bw 'Elephantine' is an island right in the middle of 𓇋𓏏𓂋𓈘𓈇𓅯𓏲 itrw Ḥʿpy 'Nile river' where, due to untold millennia of inundation, the Blackest soil would be found.

Indeed, even 𓂝𓄿𓅓𓏥 aAm.w 'eurasians' themselves (ɛ.n., greek, roman, and arab invaders, enslavers, and colonizers) – are in agreement that the land which is now known as "Afrika", whose original people, the authochtones, were not pale eurasians, but were rather indigenous Black people. Thus, the name for the land is derived from the people and not vice-versa as seen in example (9):

9.
a. Greek: Αἰθιοπία Aethiopia 'Land of burnt faces (Blacks)' as in the modern country of Ethiopia
b. Latin: Niger 'Black'
c. Arabic: بلاد السودان Bilad as Sudan 'Land of the Blacks'

Another major point that should be reconsidered is the use of the term 𓆎𓅓𓏏𓊖 Kmt 'The Black Nation/Land of the Blacks' rather than "Africa." The name 𓆎𓅓𓏏𓊖 Kmt 'The Black Nation/Land of the Blacks' itself is useful because it identifies a link between the land and the people and vice versa. On the other hand, however, gaining greater use after the defeat of ˣʷᴬᴴ⁻ˣᑫᶲ Qart-ḥadašt 'Carthage' after the third punic war, the etymologically opaque and relatively meaningless term "Africa" is a case of synechdoche or pars pro toto whereby the name give n to a small part of something comes to be identified with the larger whole. However, we note that

All Black People Look Alike: Ethnicity & Language

'Provincia Africa Proconsularis' amounted to little more than a thin strip of coastal land as shown in Figure 2.[xiv]

Moreover, it was the term used to describe rome's defeated and incorporated province. Needless to say, any free and/or self-determining people would be unwilling to accept a name connoting a defeated strip of land annexed by the roman republic. However, in accepting such a self-defeating name, self-defeating attitudes and behaviors are likely to follow. As a proverb in Kiswahili states Ukirithi jina urithi na mambo yake "If you inherit a name you must also adopt its affairs."[xv]

As such, it should be clear that our classical identity is as 𓆎𓅓𓏏𓏥 Kmt(yw) 'Black People' rather than the divisions with which we now identify. In the words of Maam Seex Anta Jóob (Cheikh Anta Diop):

> We need to distinguish two levels: the immediate one of local histories, so dear, deeply lived, in which the Afrikan peoples, segmented, by diverse exterior forces the principle one of which is colonization, are shriveled up, find themselves trapped, and are vegetating today. A second level, more general, further off in time and space and including the totality of our peoples, comprises the general history of Black Africa.[xvi]

In a similar vein, we should note here that the term Yorùbá, with which millions of people now identify, is not even indigenous to the Yorùbá and was used as an exonym by the Hausa/Fulani to refer to those who spoke a large swath of mutually intelligible languages as 'shady and unreliable.'[xvii] This begs the question of how can we self-identify as a concept that did not even exist when our Ancestors were stolen as the term itself is only first

Figure 2: The making of mud bricks from the Black soil of Ȝbw (Elephantine) island

Figure 3: Provincia Africa Proconsularis highlighed in red (Image credit: Milenioscuro)

attested in 1829 in the work of Clapperton, where he writes "We learned in fact that we were not now in the king of Badagry's territory, but in a district of Eyeo, which is called Yarriba by the Arabs and people of Houssa."[xviii] This use was reinforced by Bishop Samuel Ajàyí Crowther on a mission to Nigeria in 1841 who decided to take up the exonym to refer to mutually intelligible dialects.[xix] Thus began the adoption and entrenchment of "Yorùbá" as a name with his later publication on Yorùbá grammar.[xx]

Similarly, while non-Blacks came to the area now known as Ghana back in 1471 CE, the first known use of the term Akan was in 1694 CE—well over two hundred (200) years later—and it did not gain currency as a supposed ethnonym until the 1950s when linguists decided to use it as "an umbrella term to describe the language of the people."[xxi] Indeed, while many are aware of the Berlin Conference 1884-1885 CE, at which 𓀀𓀁𓂀 ı ı ꜣmw 'foreigners (from

Figure 4: Languages of Black People as 𓀀 Gabriel conceived of by ꜣmw 'foreigners (from eurasia)' linguists and as followed by pretty much everyone else. Notice how these divisions are similar to those of the Berlin Conference, which operates on the same CT ontological (mis-)understanding

All Black People Look Alike: Ethnicity & Language

eurasia)' divided the land of Black people politically, comparatively less people are aware of a similar process in which contemporary 𓀁𓂋𓀠 ⲙⲙⲱ 'foreigners (from eurasia)' linguists turned cultural-linguistic groups into "tribes" (now known euphemistically as ethnic groups) based on their language and the mutual intelligibility or lack thereof vis-à-vis neighboring languages.[xxii] This linguistically-based "tribification" is based on the so-called Classical Theory (CT).

Visit Repatriate to Ghana>>>>>>>

The classical theory which goes back to Aristotle, classifies entities according to necessary and sufficient conditions. This means that a certain category, for example, is defined by specific features; and each of the features is considered necessary for the definition of that category. For an entity to be said to belong to that category it must have all of the defining features of that category, otherwise it cannot be put in that category. The sufficiency of the defining features lies in the fact that an entity can be considered to belong to the category if it possesses each defining feature of the category.[xxiii]

Essentially, this inappropriate conception of reality introduces a fiction in which there is a sharp dividing line between one "tribe/ethnic group" and the other as demonstrated in Figures 3 and 4:[xxiv]

However, it has been observed that, to the contrary, "Although logic may treat categories as though membership is all or none, natural languages themselves possess linguistic mechanisms for coding and coping with gradients of category membership"[xxv]

This gradient-based conception of reality is vastly different than one that categorizes on the basis of sharp dividing lines between one category (in this case language) and another. Such an alternative understanding can be demonstrated in Figure 5:

All Black People Look Alike: Ethnicity & Language

Figure 5: Linguistically delineated and defined "tribes" as incorrectly conceptualized by modern day ꜣmw 'foreigners (from eurasia)' linguists based on a CT-based ontological misinterpretation of reality

As alluded to above, even the labels with which we now identify, in many cases were not conceptualized nor developed by us. Secondarily, even if they were, the reality is that related languages—particularly at points of confluence—share features and aspects that a CT necessary-and-sufficient-conditions-based mis-understanding of reality obscures. Even when ꜣmw 'foreigners (from eurasia)' linguists and their ostensibly Black lackeys are willing to concede to lump the languages of contemporary Kmt(yw) 'Black People' into larger groupings, it is still on the basis of Classical Theory with its sharp dividing lines as shown in Figure 4.

However, even these "supertribes" may not stand up to scientific scrutiny; particularly when we see the same basic vocabulary that cuts across supposedly mutually exclusive categorial membership—pointing to a common origin/source of the languages in question that are painted as belonging to different families. World-renowned scholar and linguist Tâta Théophile Obenga shows just such a situation whereby languages from supposedly different families share the same word across the length and breadth of the continent.

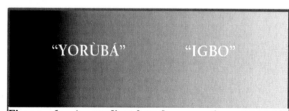

Figure 6: A gradient-based conception, more in alignment with the confluence of mutual intelligibility and areal distribution of linguistic features vis-à-vis supposedly mutually exclusive language groupings

The sheer spatial and temporal depth involved makes the idea that they borrowed the word from one supposed "language family" to another highly unlikely. It rather

All Black People Look Alike: Ethnicity & Language

points to a common ancestral proto-language from which they are all descended. Just such an illustrative case is shown below:

10.

Table 2: Putative cognates from supposedly different language families pointing to a common source language from which they are all descended.[xxvi]

Language	Supposed Language Family	Word		
Mdw Ntr 'Hieroglyphs'	Afro-Asiatic	bìn 'mal' (wrong)		
		bìn 'mauvais' (bad)		
Coptic	Afro-Asiatic	ⲃⲟⲟⲛⲉ /boonĕ/ 'mal' (wrong)		
		ⲃⲁⲁⲛⲉ /baanĕ/ 'mal' (wrong)		
		ⲃⲟⲛⲓ /bonĕ/ 'mauvais' (bad)		
		ⲃⲁⲛⲓ /banĕ/ 'mauvais' (bad)		
Matakam	Afro-Asiatic	ba 'mal/mauvais' (wrong/bad)		
Mboku	Afro-Asiatic	bay 'mal/mauvais' (wrong/bad)		
Hurza	Afro-Asiatic	ba 'mal/mauvais' (wrong/bad)		
Songhay	Nilo-Saharan	bone 'mal' wrong'		
Kanuri	Nilo-Saharan	bûì 'bad luck'		
Bambara	Niger-Congo A	bone 'malheur' (misfortune)		
Asante	Niger-Congo A	bɔne 'bad'		
Peul	Niger-Congo A	bone 'wickedness'		
Wolof	Niger-Congo A	bon		

Yorùbá	Niger-Congo A	ibi 'evil'
Lyele	Niger-Congo A	byena 'mal/mauvais' (wrong/bad)
Kaje	Niger-Congo A	biyin 'mauvais' (bad)
Tunen	Niger-Congo B	-bɛ 'wrong'
Lingala	Niger-Congo B	mabé 'bad'
Kiswahili	Niger-Congo B	mbaya 'bad'
IsiZulu	Niger-Congo B	-bi 'evil, bad, wicked, wrong, nasty'
Kikôngo	Niger-Congo B	mbi 'bad, wrong, evil'

Study African languages w/ Abibitum>>>>>>

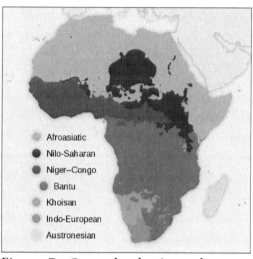

Figure 7: Currently dominant language family model

The above exercise utilizes just one example of the 105 putative cognates identified by Tâta Théophile Obenga that cut across so-called language families.[xxvii] Thus, it is readily apparent that the currently dominant language-family model obscures the fact that all of the languages listed in Table 1 are ultimately descended from the same proto-language, referred to by Tâta Théophile Obenga as Négro-Égyptien 'Black-Egyptian'—the source language of all Kmt(yw) 'Black People'.

This scenario is akin to a single river with many branches that may separate only to reunite further downstream—but ultimately

All Black People Look Alike: Ethnicity & Language

belonging to just one river—regardless of the arbitrary Berlin-conference-like divisions externally imposed upon them.

Ultimately, there is the question of perspective whereby one may choose to emphasize the distributaries/rivulets or the river. I note here, however, that whether 𓂋𓏥 ḫmw 'foreigners (from eurasia)' linguists and their anti-Black lackeys choose to emphasize the oneness or the diversity, they do so with the interests of 𓂋𓏥 ḫmw 'foreigners (from eurasia)' in mind.

Nonetheless, I note that even fabrications can be brought into being in the minds of people (with implications with regard to lived reality) and must be addressed appropriately.

So, what does this all have to do with repatriation? Well, ultimately, one can choose to identify with the river or the distributaries/rivulets.

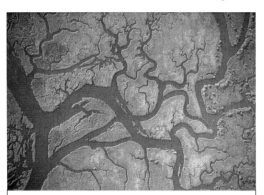

Figure 8: Like a river, even when languages separate, they are still connected as one even when land apparently intervenes between one distributary and another.

We can choose to be 𓆎𓅓𓏏𓏤 Kmt(yw) 'Black People' or we can choose to be fragments. We can choose to see the gradients between us or to see sharp dividing lines and their concomitant compartmentalization and dichotomization. As our "Yorùbá"-speaking Ancestors relate: Ohun t'ojú ń wá l'ojú ń rí 'What the eye is looking for, is what the eye is seeing.' In other words, your perspective and intentionality behind that perspective may shape what you conceptualize and/or realize as the nature of being/existence.

All Black People Look Alike: Ethnicity & Language

With regard to repatriation, interestingly, in the last Right to Return Last Town Hall Meeting for 2020, my good friend and colleague Dr. Hamet Maulana gave a spirited talk calling for Diasporans to come to see themselves as one of many tribes in Ghana, with its own interests and pursuits.

As this was going on, in the live chat discussion, at the 2:44:07 mark you can clearly see a conversation between user antseif and C Jh, where antseif commented "well I thought the diaspora were going to unite us continental Africans so we could get rid of tribalism which is impeding progress but NOT form another tribe to further deepen our problems [...]We don't want more divisions...Dr Maulana...NO MORE TRIBES..."

Figure 9: Screenshot of Live Chat Replay from the MoF Town Hall Meeting

To which user C Jh replied "@antseif I was having the same debate, it feels a little separatist to me also. I thought the idea was to move back home and become part of the family again not set up another one."

In classical times, we had those who worked towards us seeing ourselves on the basis of what we have in common, being Kmt(yw) 'Black People' and we had those who worked towards us seeing ourselves as innumerable fragments. An analogous situation pertains now.

As such, when you repatriate to Ghana, I would encourage you to not only learn more than one language, but to learn languages from throughout the continent. Just last month I returned to the neo-colonial cage known as Ghana from the neo-colonial cage known as Nigeria have had intellectual conversations in "Yorùbá" about the nature of prefixes in "Akan," "Yorùbá," "Wolof," and "Bantu languages" and how nominalization markers in "Yorùbá" may be vestigial noun class markers. I had scholarly debates in "Yorùbá" on whether or not èsìn 'religion' is an indigenous concept, continuous vs. discontinuous revelation, the nature of Olódùmarè, n.k. The only reason why I was able to do in "Yorùbá" what I regularly do in "Akan" was because I know that we are all 𓂋𓅓𓏏𓏥 Kmt(yw) 'Black People'. If I thought I was "Akan" or if I thought I was Ghanaian or if I thought I was "Yorùbá" or "Nigerian", the limited diameter of such an understanding would have implications for the circumference of my possibilities as it is, unfortunately, rare for 𓂋𓅓𓏏𓏥 Kmt(yw) 'Black People' of contemporary times to be able to master other indigenous languages outside of their specific neo-colonial cages.

In short, our behavior is directly attributable to who we say we are. Our possibilities are governed by our identities. When you repatriate to Ghana or elsewhere in contemporary 𓆎𓅓𓏏𓊖 Kmt 'The Black Nation/Land of the Blacks' you also have the choice to focus on the river or focus on the rivulet. One should choose wisely.

Part and parcel of the services that we offer is a series of consultations aimed at assisting and guiding contemporary 𓂋𓅓𓏏𓏥 Kmt(yw) 'Black People' interested in repatriating to the continent of contemporary 𓆎𓅓𓏏𓊖 Kmt 'The Black Nation/Land of the Blacks'; this is in its broadest sense and with the original understanding that all land of 𓂋𓅓𓏏𓏥 Kmt(yw) 'Black People' is rightfully 𓆎𓅓𓏏𓊖 Kmt 'The Black Nation/Land of the Blacks'—including those currently criminally occupied by 𓀀𓀁𓏪 ꜥmw 'foreigners (from eurasia)' and/or divided into neo-colonial fragments. While the land of Black people has been fragmented into neo-colonial cages, the

All Black People Look Alike: Ethnicity & Language

restoration efforts are underway and your repatriation serves as an integral piece of the puzzle to bring us back to the state of Abibitumi (Black Power) necessary to do so. Interested in playing your part? Sign up for an initial consultation to see if Repatriate to Ghana is a good fit for you and what you envision for your future and for the beautyful ones not yet born. **Take the Repatriation Quiz>>>>>>>>**

References

Allen, James Peter. The Ancient Egyptian Pyramid Texts. Writings from the Ancient World. Edited by Peter Der Manuelian. Atlanta: The Society of Biblical Literature, 2005.

Blackman, Aylward M, and Michael R Apted. The Rock Tombs of Meir, Part V. Edited by Raymond O. Faulkner. London: Oxford University Press, 1953.

Clapperton, Hugh. Journal of a Second Expedition into the Interior of Africa: From the Bight of Benin to Soccatoo. Philadelphia, PA: Carey, Lea and Carey, 1829.

Crowther, S. A Vocabulary of the Yoruba Language, Compiled by the Rev. Samuel Crowther ... Together with Introductory Remarks, by the Rev. O.E. Vidal. London: Seeleys, 1852.
https://books.google.com.gh/books?id=fg7nQwAACAAJ.

Diop, Cheikh Anta. Civilization or Barbarism: An Authentic Anthropology. Translated by Yaa-Lengi Meema Ngemi. Edited by Harold J. Salemson and Marjolijn de Jager. Chicago: Lawrence Hill Books, 1981.

Diop, Cheikh Anta, and Theophile Obenga. The Origin of the Ancient Egyptians. The Peopling of Ancient Egypt and the Deciphering of Meroitic Script: Unesco's the General History of Africa Studies and Documents, I and Ii. London: Karnak House, 1978.

Dolphyne, Florence Abena. The Akan (Twi-Fante) Language: Its Sound System and Tonal Structure. Accra: Ghana Universities Press, 1988.

Faulkner, Raymond O. "A Concise Dictionary of Middle Egyptian." Oxford: Griffith Institute, 1962.

Gabliang. "Major Languages in Africa 2019." Languages in Africa. Web: reddit.com, 19 November 2019 2019.
https://www.reddit.com/r/MapPorn/comments/dw9kdr/oc_major_african_lan guages_in_2019/.

"Yoruba Leaders Disagree over Origin, Meaning of Their Name." vanguardngr.com, 2019, accessed 12 April 2021, 2021, https://www.vanguardngr.com/2019/10/yoruba-leaders-disagree-over-origin-meaning-of-their-name/.

Kambon, Ọ. The Akan Language. 2002. African Languages and Literature, University of Wisconsin-Madison, Madison, WI.

All Black People Look Alike: Ethnicity & Language

Kambon, Ọ., and Yaw Mankatah Asare. "Humanities and Sciences as Complementary Aspects of an Afrikan=Black Whole: Evidence from Archeoastronomy." Legon Journal of the Humanities 30, no. 2 (2019): 215-42. https://www.ajol.info/index.php/ljh/article/view/195066/184243.

Kambon, Ọbádélé, and Roland Mireku Yeboah. "What Afrikan Names May (or May Not) Tell Us About the State of Pan-Afrikanism." Journal of Black Studies 50, no. 6 (2019): 569–601. https://doi.org/https://doi.org/10.1177/0021934719867923.

Kasser, Rodolphe, and Philippe Luisier. "P. Bodmer XI: "Cantique Des Cantiques" En Copte Saïdique." Orientalia 81, no. 3 (2012): 149-201. www.jstor.org/stable/43077429.

Lake, Edward John. The Church Missionary Atlas: Containing an Account of the Various Countries in Which the Church Missionary Society Labours, and of Its Missionary Operations. London: Church Missionary House, 1879.

Lakoff, George. Women, Fire and Dangerous Things. Chicago: University of Chicago Press, 1987.

Laman, Karl Edvard. Dictionnaire Kikongo-Français. Vol. 2, Upper Saddle River, NJ: Gregg Press, 1964.

Maiga, Hassimi. Conversational Songhoy Language of Mali (West Africa). New Orleans: Muhrem Books, 1996. http://www.coribe.org/SONGHOY/Pages/overview.html#black.

Milenioscuro. "Locator Map of the Africa Proconsularis Province in the Roman Empire ". Web: Wikimedia Commons, 17 November 2015 2015. https://commons.wikimedia.org/wiki/File:Roman_Empire_-_Africa_Proconsularis_(125_AD).svg.

Nwachukwu, P.A., O. Ndimele, and Linguistic Association of Nigeria. Trends in the Study of Languages and Linguistics in Nigeria. Port Harcourt: Grand Orbit Communications & Emhai Press, 2005. https://books.google.com.gh/books?id=StZhAAAAMAAJ.

Obenga, Theophile. Origine Commune De L'egyptien Ancien, Du Copte Et Des Langues Negro-Africaines Modernes. Paris: L'Harmattan, 1993.

Osam, E. Kweku. "Aspects of Akan Grammar: A Functional Perspective." Ph.D. Thesis, University of Oregon, 1994.

Prah, Kwesi Kwaa. "Mother-Tongue Education in Africa for Emancipation and Development: Towards the Intellectualisation of African Languages." Languages and education in Africa: A comparative and transdisciplinary analysis (2009): 83-104.

Rosch, Eleanor. "Principles of Categorization ". In Cognition and Categorization, edited by E Rosch and B. B. Lloyd, 27-48. Hillsdale, NJ: Erlbaum, 1978.

Salami, G., M.B. Visona, and D. Arnold. A Companion to Modern African Art. Hoboken, NJ: Wiley, 2013. https://books.google.com.gh/books?id=fZZxDwAAQBAJ.

Sauneron, Serge. Le Temple D'esna. Vol. III, Le Caire: Institut Français d'Archéologie Orientale, coll.«ESNA», 1968.

Sethe, Kurt. Die Altägyptischen Pyramidentexte Nach Den Papierabdrücken Und Photographien Des Berliner Museums. Leipzig: J.C. Hinrichs'sche Buchhandlung, 1910. https://books.google.com.gh/books?id=8eHkAAAAMAAJ.

All Black People Look Alike: Ethnicity & Language

---

i James Peter Allen, The Ancient Egyptian Pyramid Texts, ed. Peter Der Manuelian, Writings from the ancient world, (Atlanta: The Society of Biblical Literature, 2005)., p. 127. Kurt Sethe, Die Altägyptischen Pyramidentexte nach den Papierabdrücken und Photographien des Berliner Museums (Leipzig: J.C. Hinrichs'sche Buchhandlung, 1910). https://books.google.com.gh/books?id=8ehkAAAAMAAJ., §1998.

ii Aylward M Blackman and Michael R Apted, The Rock Tombs of Meir, Part V, ed. Raymond O. Faulkner (London: Oxford University Press, 1953)., plate XIV.

iii Rodolphe Kasser and Philippe Luisier, "P. Bodmer XL: "Cantique des Cantiques" en copte saïdique," Orientalia 81, no. 3 (2012), www.jstor.org/stable/43077429.

iv Bibi is also Black in the Songhoy language of Mali, where it retains its deep philosophical, cosmological, and ontological connotations. cf. Hassimi Maiga, Conversational Songhoy Language of Mali (West Africa) (New Orleans: Muhrem Books, 1996). http://www.coribe.org/SONGHOY/Pages/overview.html#black.

v G. Salami, M.B. Visona, and D. Arnold, A Companion to Modern African Art (Hoboken, NJ: Wiley, 2013). https://books.google.com.gh/books?id=fZZxDwAAQBAJ., p. 546.

vi Karl Edvard Laman, Dictionnaire kikongo-français, vol. 2 (Upper Saddle River, NJ: Gregg Press, 1964)., p. 672.

vii Thanks to Dr. Chika Mba for pointing this term out to me.

viii Ndi nna P.A. Nwachukwu, O. Ndimele, and Linguistic Association of Nigeria, Trends in the study of languages and linguistics in Nigeria (Port Harcourt: Grand Orbit Communications & Emhai Press, 2005). https://books.google.com.gh/books?id=StZhAAAAMAAJ., pp. 425, 433.

ix Raymond O. Faulkner, "A Concise Dictionary of Middle Egyptian," (Oxford: Griffith Institute, 1962)., p. 286.

x Nananom Cheikh Anta Diop and Theophile Obenga, The Origin of the Ancient Egyptians, The Peopling of Ancient Egypt and the Deciphering of Meroitic Script: UNESCO's The General History of Africa Studies and Documents, I and II., (London: Karnak House, 1978)., p. 27.

xi Q. Kambon and Yaw Mankatah Asare, "Humanities and Sciences as Complementary Aspects of an Afrikan=Black Whole: Evidence from Archeoastronomy," Legon Journal of the Humanities 30, no. 2 (2019), https://www.ajol.info/index.php/ljh/article/view/195066/184243.

xii Cf. Faulkner, "A Concise Dictionary of Middle Egyptian.", p. 286.

xiii Serge Sauneron, Le Temple d'Esna, vol. III (Le Caire: Institut Français d'Archéologie Orientale, coll.«ESNA», 1968)., p. 132.

xiv Milenioscuro, "Locator map of the Africa Proconsularis province in the Roman Empire " (Web: Wikimedia Commons, 17 November 2015 2015). https://commons.wikimedia.org/wiki/File:Roman_Empire_-_Africa_Proconsularis_(125_AD).svg.

xv Ọbádélé Kambon and Roland Mireku Yeboah, "What Afrikan Names may (or may not) Tell Us about the State of Pan-Afrikanism," Journal of Black Studies 50, no. 6 (2019), https://doi.org/https://doi.org/10.1177/0021934719867923.

xvi Cheikh Anta Diop, Civilization or Barbarism: An Authentic Anthropology, trans. Yaa-Lengi Meema Ngemi, ed. Harold J. Salemson and Marjolijn de Jager (Chicago: Lawrence Hill Books, 1981)., p. 213.

xvii "Yoruba leaders disagree over origin, meaning of their name," vanguardngr.com, 2019, accessed 12 April 2021, 2021, https://www.vanguardngr.com/2019/10/yoruba-leaders-disagree-over-origin-meaning-of-their-name/.

xviii Hugh Clapperton, Journal of a Second Expedition into the Interior of Africa: from the Bight of Benin to Soccatoo (Philadelphia, PA: Carey, Lea and Carey, 1829)., p. 4.

xix Edward John Lake, The Church Missionary Atlas: Containing an Account of the Various Countries in which the Church Missionary Society Labours, and of Its Missionary Operations (London: Church Missionary House, 1879).

xx S. Crowther, A Vocabulary of the Yoruba Language, Compiled by the Rev. Samuel Crowther ... Together with Introductory Remarks, by the Rev. O.E. Vidal (London: Seeleys, 1852). https://books.google.com.gh/books?id=fg7nQwAACAAJ.

xxi Ọ Kambon, The Akan Language, 2002, African Languages and Literature, University of Wisconsin-Madison, Madison, WI., p. 4. Florence Abena Dolphyne, The Akan (Twi-Fante) Language: Its Sound System and Tonal Structure. (Accra: Ghana Universities Press, 1988)., p. xi.

xxii Kwesi Kwaa Prah, "Mother-tongue education in Africa for emancipation and development: Towards the intellectualisation of African languages," Languages and education in Africa: A comparative and transdisciplinary analysis (2009).

xxiii For a succinct, yet thorough discussion of the classical theory see Osam "Aspects of Akan Grammar: A Functional Perspective" (Ph.D. Thesis, University of Oregon, 1994)., p. 10., and Lakoff Women, Fire and Dangerous Things (Chicago: University of Chicago Press, 1987)..

All Black People Look Alike: Ethnicity & Language

xxiv Gabliang, "Major Languages in Africa 2019," (Web: reddit.com, 19 November 2019 2019). https://www.reddit.com/r/MapPorn/comments/dw9kdr/oc_major_african_languages_in_2019/.

xxv Eleanor Rosch, "Principles of categorization " in Cognition and categorization, ed. E Rosch and B. B. Lloyd (Hillsdale, NJ: Erlbaum, 1978)., p. 39.

xxvi Adapted from Theophile Obenga, Origine Commune de l'Egyptien Ancien, du Copte et des Langues Negro-Africaines Modernes (Paris: L'Harmattan, 1993)., pp. 286-287.

xxvii Obenga, Origine Commune de l'Egyptien Ancien, du Copte et des Langues Negro-Africaines Modernes.

Check out Black Classic Press

CHOP LIFE: FOOD & DIET

Let me start this chapter properly by saying that Ghana Jollof is number one! Do not make the mistake of asking a Ghanaian if their Jollof is better than Nigerian Jollof. I love Ghanaian food. The food is worth repatriating alone. But before we talk about the actual food and some of my favorite dishes, let's talk a little but about food culture and agriculture.

<<<<<<<<Learn to Make Jollof Rice

Sunday dinner is definitely an African concept. Black families of all socioeconomic positions understand the importance and value of sitting down and having a meal together. Whether it's a mayonnaise sandwich or steak and lobster, we are sitting down, praying over our food, and eating together. Ghanaians like many other African people, practice eating out of a community plate. Having a meal is more than bodily nourishment-- it's spiritual. Expect to be offered to share a meal. It may be someone's personal dish. They may only have a little bit but they will say "you are welcome" and they mean it. When you're offered, say yes and watch what happens.

Agriculture

In Ghana the agricultural sector consists of crops, livestock, fisheries, and the cocoa sectors. Agriculture is vital to the overall economic growth and development of Ghana and it accounts for over 50% of the country's GDP. Cocoa accounts for about 20% of Ghana's agriculture and about half of the country's total cultivated land area is used for cocoa. The bulk of farmers are small farm holders accounting for about 80% of the agricultural production with the average farm size less than 1.5 hectares.

Chop Life: Food & Diet

<<<<<<<Learn about our Cocoa Project

Subsistence farming is very common in rural areas. Productivity is fairly low mainly because many farmers don't have the resources required to maintain their farms and maximize their yield.

Ghana's main food crops include maize, yam, cassava, cocoyam, plantain, rice, sorghum, millet and other root crops. The main cash crops include cocoa, beans, palm, pineapples, cotton, bananas, mangoes, citrus fruits, coconuts, tobacco, cashew, groundnuts, rubber, sugar cane and fresh vegetables. Cotton production is mostly concentrated in the three northern regions.

Commonly cultivated vegetables include eggplant (garden eggs), tomato, okra, beans, shallots, spinach, sweet pepper, and chili pepper. Other vegetables grown in-country include carrots, cucumber, squash, pumpkin, cabbage, lettuce, cauliflower, chayote, bottle gourd, kontomire, vegetable sponge, coconut palm, eddoes, bitter leaf, sesame, and green beans. Tomato is undoubtedly the most important vegetable in Ghana . Grains grown in Ghana include wheat, rice, maize, sorghum, millet. Legumes – or beans - include cowpea, soybean, groundnut, chickpeas, peanuts and tamarind.

Because of the variety of climate zones ranging from dry savannas to wet forests, a lot of different fruits grow in Ghana including oranges, bananas, African pears, lemons, limes, noni fruit, sisibi, tangerines, soursop pineapples, mangoes, papayas, melons, coconut, guavas, atemoya, jackfruit, pears, watermelons, african star, avocadoes, cashew, dates, velvet tamarind and tropical almonds. There is no shortage of delicious and fresh fruit anywhere in Ghana.

Chop Life: Food & Diet

Ghana has less of a problem with crop production than it does with processing raw goods into consumable products. As a result, many products are exported, and then return to Ghana as imported, packaged goods. Ghana's agricultural sector is ripe with opportunities for Black farmers who've mastered contemporary farming with updated technology to collaborate with local farmers. This could easily help Ghana increase the quantity and quality of its crop production, and could attract more African Americans to the food processing business.

Research Ghana Agricultural Data>>>>>>>

As you read in the previous chapter, Ghana is made up of several ethnic groups with diverse cultures and food is a major aspect of culture. The Ghanaian diet relies largely on starchy staple foods which go with a sauce or soup containing protein, fruits, and vegetables. The average traditional Ghanaian meal is heavy. Ghanaians love Ghanaian food and they don't play around with their food. It's serious business.

Eating with your hands is also commonplace - the right hand to be specific. In many African cultures, every function dealing with food, greetings and passing things is done with the right hand. The left hand is traditionally used to clean oneself after a bowel movement. And I'm not talking about with toilet tissue, a relatively new invention.

Although modern kitchens with stoves exist, many Ghanaians still have outdoor kitchens and prefer to cook over wood or coals. In some instances, it's more about economics than anything else. A lot of people don't have stoves as we know them. I'm partial to having food cooked outdoors over the open fire. as I think it simply tastes better.

Because of Ghana's climate allows so many things to grow, the diet is most often based on what's plenty and available in a specific place or during a certain season. Cassava, plantain and maize

Chop Life: Food & Diet

grow everywhere. These are also the main ingredients in the base of many Ghanaian meals (or two Ghanaian staples) fufu and banku.

Fufu is boiled cassava pounded into a thick dough-like consistency that's often mixed with boiled plantain. It's a manual process that takes time and labor but can feed an army fairly inexpensively because it's free It's often served with light soup which- a tomato-based broth blended with pepper, ginger, garlic, other local spices and a choice of meat. It sounds pretty simple but all Fufu and light soup are not created equal. The entire process is special and a science.

Maize is the base for banku and akeple. Banku is fermented corn that is dried, ground, boiled and mixed with a large wooden spoon while cooking over fire. It's then shaped and wrapped in a plantain leaf. Akeple and banku have similar processes. A Ghanaian favorite is banku and tilapia – a dish consisting of grilled tilapia, banku and an assortment of fresh ground wet pepper, sliced tomato and onion. Delicious is an understatement.

Check out Naomi's Firepot >>>>>>>>>>>>

The traditional Ghanaian diet aligns with a traditionally physically active lifestyle.
Ghanaians typically rise early in the morning to complete the strenuously laborious maintenance of land. Farmers and their families walk long distances and expend tremendous energy to complete simple tasks in the blazing sun. Fueling these efforts require significant sustenance before and/or after.

Some breakfast diets include koko with koose, rice water (rice porridge), millet porridge, maize porridge or fermented maize porridge. Some other traditional and popular Ghanaian foods include akpele with okra stew, kenkey (komi/dokonu) with pepper, tuazafi, fonfom, kokonte with groundnut soup, akyeke,

Chop Life: Food & Diet

mpotompoto, waakye, red-red (beans with fried plantain), omo tua (rice balls) with soup, kelewele, boiled yam/plantain with kotonmire, garden egg stew (eggplant stew), angwa mo (oiled rice), aprapransa, plakali, tubani, boiled coco yam with grinded (ground) pepper or stew, and of course Jollof rice.

Meat is large part of the Ghanaian diet but can also be luxury for those who can afford to have meat in every meal. Beef, lamb, chicken, and pork are prepared everywhere. The Kabob is a staple. Grilled guinea fowl is one of my favorites. I hadn't eaten any animal intestine until Ghana. My first time eating sheep intestine was also my first time cleaning sheep intestine. I am not grossed out by it at all. In fact, I often wonder how people can be grossed out by animals and still eat them. No judgment, I just don't understand it myself. Naturally, fish is a very large part of the diet. What I I love is that the meat is fresh. I normally get to see the animal alive when I'm in the village before it becomes a part of the meal. It's standard for us to pray over the animal before it is processed, as opposed to purchasing packaged meat from a grocery store which, more often than not, is filled with all types of drugs and chemicals. Meats are free-range and organic, for the most part.

Vegetables are often a part of Ghanaian traditional meals, but not very often the main dish. I love vegetables and salads. If you're a real Black person, you couldn't go outside, play a game, or get up from the dinner table until you finished your vegetables. Vegetables one of our four basic food groups. I do miss having vegetables as a regular part of meals. Spinach, broccoli and broccolini, green beans, collard, kale, and mustard greens, cauliflower, and cabbage are some of my favorites. So I hope to grow them in Ghana. I also love a great salad. Salads are hard to come by unless you're at restaurant and it's on the menu or you make your own. If having vegetables as part of your daily diet is important, you're going to have to make an effort.

Chop Life: Food & Diet

More and more people are opting for a vegetarian, vegan or plant-based lifestyle, globally. While vegetarian and vegan restaurants are not as plentiful, there are a few and more popping up. With the increasing number of expats, you find more and more vegetarian and vegan options. You can easily and inexpensively live a vegan and vegetarian lifestyle in Ghana.

Accra and greater Accra is a metropolitan area so you will find a wide array of available foods and restaurants beyond traditional Ghanaian food. Other regions and areas don't have as many options as Accra but the restaurant scene in Accra is popping and every day you will find new restaurants.

While Ghana has a newly emerging restaurant and dining culture, customer service generally is poor. Most of the fine dining establishments many expats and diasporans frequent will have better customer service. Customer service training and standards are areas of improvement where I believe Ghana needs to create a strong uncompromised focus. As a repatriate, this is where you have to bring your patience and make an early decision to not allow these inevitable hiccups to color your entire experience. Don't let the taste of the poor customer service taint the taste of your food.

Unlike popular characterizations that Africa is just poor with starving people, you'll probably put on weight and eat more than you do at home. Your food and diet will also have an impact on your health because as the saying goes, we are what we eat. I believe in doing my best to live a preventative lifestyle and avoid ailments or sickness that can often be tied to what and how we eat. In the next chapter we'll discuss health care so if you do find yourself needing medical attention, you can have an understanding what to expect. But focusing on your food and diet will help you keep your medical challenges and emergencies to a minimum.
Some of my favorite places to eat>>>>>>>

HEALTH CARE: HOSPITALS & INSURANCE

Writing this book has encouraged me to do what I am suggesting for you – make sure you have an emergency health care plan in place for you and your family. Health care is extremely important. Having access to trained, knowledgeable doctors and equipped up to date technologically advanced hospitals, for everyday life and emergencies is often one of the global barometers for what a developed nation looks like. And it's a major factor in deciding where you should repatriate. As mentioned previously, Ghana offers the ability to eat freshly grown foods, walk more and eat less processed foods encouraging a more preventative lifestyle.

If there's one thing Africa and Ghana in particular have shown the world during this Pandemic, is that America is not always the safest place. Ghana handled the pandemic extremely well by all standards so any challenges around health care in Ghana are not based on ability or capacity rather priority, finances and infrastructure.

Ghana also has many traditional herbs and plants as remedies for various ailments, so contemporary pharmaceutical medicine is not always the best answer alone. Sometimes you may need to go to the hospital and use a natural supplement.

I contracted malaria in 2020. It was my first time personally experiencing malaria although you'll find a lot of people have malaria and deal with it every day. I was lucky to detect it very early as I am learning to listen to my body. At the time I went to Koforidua Hospital, which is the closest to Nyame Bekyre, I couldn't keep any food down and suffered with bad diarrhea. I spent 2 days in the hospital. I don't even know what drugs they gave me but I wanted everything they had in the strongest dosage. After two days I was discharged. However, it was the herbal remedies that helped me get my strength and vim back. Neem is a natural herb that grows everywhere in Ghana and many Ghanaians use it to treat malaria. We have a tree in our compound. After returning from the hospital, I took a series of neem steam baths.

Check out my neem steam bath>>>>>>>>>

Sickness is also not always assumed to be physical in Ghana. Spiritual sickness is often a viable reason for some sort of physical or mental challenge. Ghana is home to many traditional spiritual healers and many people use them. Seeking a spiritual healer should be just as careful and a selective process as choosing a medical doctor if not more. My suggestion is to start with a verified recommendation from someone who is familiar and has had great results.

Ghana's Healthcare System

In Ghana most people access health care from government-funded facilities such as the regional, district or community hospitals. Regional hospitals will have many facilities and treat more complex health issues than the district and community hospitals. The Ghanaian government's health service mission statement includes the goals of:

- Management and administration of the overall health resources within the service
- Promoting healthy mode of living and good health habits
- Establishing effective mechanisms for disease surveillance, prevention and control

These goals are to be supported by both public and private health providers. Ghanaian residents are automatically enrolled in Ghana's National Health Insurance Scheme (NHIS). Expats and non-residents can enroll at a small fee. With this insurance, a

Health Care: Hospitals & Insurance

typical visit to a general practitioner will cost around US $11.00. NHIS covers a variety of outpatient, in-patient, oral health, eye care, maternity care, and emergency services.

<<<<<<Visit Ghana Health Service

There are a number of private health providers but these medical professionals are more expensive, and many Ghanaians cannot afford the services. The health insurance business is unfamiliar to the ordinary Ghanaian as the commonly used provider is the National Health Insurance.

Hospitals and Medical Facilities

The majority of public hospitals in Ghana provide generalized services. There are around 1,800 public hospitals in Ghana, inclusive of medical facilities run by religious (Christian and Muslim) organizations, which are typically found in rural areas. Specialized treatment often requires travel abroad.

There are approximately 1,300 private hospitals in Ghana. These facilities typically cater to expats or those Ghanaian citizens who want access to higher standards of treatment, better-equipped medical facilities, and more emergency care options. Most also elect to enroll in some sort of international health insurance plan, as they typically provide emergency evacuation as part of their policies.

Pharmacies and Prescription Medicines

There are more than 550 pharmacies in Ghana, with most in the major cities and towns — some of which are open 24 hours. All pharmacies are not licensed to dispense all prescription medications. Repatriates should bring a healthy supply of medication for chronic conditions from their country of origin as all medications are not legal in Ghana. There are restrictions around sleeping pills, medication for ADHD and strong painkillers for which you will need a medical certificate. It is wise to create a list of the generic drug names to ensure you can access any you need. Your doctor or international private medical insurance provider will be able to help you with this.

Connect with Pure Chemists for your pharmaceutical needs>>>>>>>>>>>

Mental Health Care

While the stigma around mental health treatment in Ghana is still quite prevalent, there are a growing number of mental health facilities in larger cities, where one can find therapists, psychologists, and psychiatrists. One can access this information online, and repatriates needing these services may prefer to reach out to their international health insurer for recommendations locally.

Emergency Medical Care

DIAL 112 or 193 TO CALL AN AMBULANCE IN GHANA

Established in 2006, the National Ambulance Service (NAS) is considered one of Africa's most successful government-backed EMS development efforts. According to government reports, "Close to 60% of all Ghana's 216 districts are covered by ambulance services", many of which are located at Ghana National Fire Service stations. "Within each of Ghana's 10 regional capitals in 2013, NAS had at least 1 ambulance station and several ambulances staffed by a crew of trained EMTs." As part of the operations of the National Ambulance Service, 450 Emergency Medical Technicians (EMT) have been trained. According to the Ministry of Health, before the commissioning of the 307 ambulances in 2020, there were only 50 functioning ambulances.

This sounds really nice and reliable but the situation on the ground will prove very different. I wouldn't reply on calling an ambulance for a medical emergency. Many would agree that you are better at making sure you have a solid first aid kit and access to an available ride and driver to get yourself to the nearest hospital. Have a written emergency plan and run drills if you can especially if you have small children. Make sure everyone with and around you are clear about the plan for a medical emergency.

Emergency Medical Care

The emergency medical care field is relatively new in Ghana. In response to the death of over 100 people in a stadium trampling incident in 2001, the government of Ghana realized the need to establish a formal emergency care system. Until then, most emergency care centers were staffed by doctors who were not trained in emergency medicine. To help support the development of an emergency medical system in 2004, Ghana established the National Ambulance Service (NAS). An emergency medicine residency training program was started under the authority of the Ghana College of Surgeons and Physicians in 2009.

Licensed Private Health Insurance

The National Health Insurance Authority, the Regulator of Private Health Insurance Schemes in Ghana under the National Health Insurance Act, 2012 (Act 852), warns that apart from the listed Licensed Schemes, any other Institution, Firm, Company, or Individual(s) purporting to offer health insurance services is unlicensed and in violation of Section 63 of the National Health Insurance Act, 2012 (Act 852). Any person who transacts business with a Private Health Insurance Scheme other than those licensed in line with the above law, does so at their own risk.

Health Care: Hospitals & Insurance

In general, the health care industry is fairly new in Ghana and offers an incredible opportunity for serious health professionals. Depending on your level of awareness, preparedness and comfort, you should take all the time you need and do as much research as possible especially if you have existing conditions, small children or caring for elderly parents.

We organized some information that will be helpful in your planning>>>>>>>>

EDUCATION: THEORY & PRACTICE

All education is not created equal. Coming from a family of educators, and working with a TRIO college access program for a majority of my professional career, I've seen education from all sides. I've been a student, a teacher, a professor at the University level, and an active parent involved in my own children's education. I've seen my former students start at the bottom and make their way to doctorate degrees. And I've watched and participated with my own children as they've gone through private African centered schools in their early years, the traditional American K-12 educational system and transition into post-secondary matriculation.

Aside from innately talented or challenged children with regard to learning, my opinions and observations regarding education are consistent globally. I wholeheartedly believe that the most important actors in a child's education are their parents. Parents normally make the decisions on the educational environment, the school, education outside of the school, ownership of homework, the supporting community and serve as the ultimate accountability partners for the teacher and institution.

In my opinion, the educational process of Black children needs to be different, and from an African-centered perspective. Considering that Africa is the cradle of civilization and its ancient civilizations are the progenitors of all modern core subjects with S.T.E.A.M. focused subject areas at its center and that all world history is African history; any educational system or institution without these tenets as its foundational cornerstones, will not provide a sufficient education for a Black child. All other aspects of educational theory and practice, learning modalities and core curriculum should be built on this foundation for Black children.

Education: Theory & Practice

Most western and European colonial formal educational experiences and environments from pre-school onward exclude the contributions of Black people before the Trans-Atlantic Slave trade or contact with the European/Arab world and begin the history of Black people as subservient objects, slaves, and inherently inferior in all ways to their masters. What is taught of Africa, the land, and its ancient civilizations that gave birth to the world is gentrified, whitewashed, and historically inaccurate most times. Africa is colorfully painted as a wild barbaric jungle full of lions (...and tigers and bears oh my) with human-eating savages that were eventually saved from themselves with the introduction of "civilization" from Europeans and salvation by a white Jesus.

Articles on Black Education>>>>>>>

As many of us begin to wake up to the painful truth about our history and how we've been written out of world history - our contributions stolen and sold back to us like most museum artifacts - our search for educational truth, justice, and historical accuracy for our children has also served as fuel for our move towards repatriation to Africa. Unfortunately, African-centered education is not prominent or perpetuated in Africa, either. In fact, you'll find the flip side of the colonial educational mentality – a high degree of Stockholm Syndrome, and often just as much confusion and exclusion about the African and their contribution to the world. As a former British colony, Ghana has adopted the British educational framework, structure, and model - which is naturally counterintuitive to the development of the African child's mind.

It has been interesting for me speaking with, and learning about, my Ghanaian friends' educational experiences in Ghana, London, and the United States. They've given me their opinions of the educational system in Ghana and how/if it works as an adequate system to prepare students to fully integrate into the world. I am

Education: Theory & Practice

particularly biased towards comprehensive, well-rounded, global, and economic inclusive African-centered education with a focus on nation building for all Black children. Again, I underscore my belief that all educational systems and institutions that exclude Africa and its contributions to the world teeter between bad and worse for Black children.

<<<<<<Ghana Education Services

Educating a child in Africa, specifically in Ghana, affords you direct access to traditional culture and customs that can help you color your child's educational experience in a positive way. Traditional culture is inescapable in daily Ghanaian life unless you work to avoid it or exclude it from your lifestyle. Most immediately through language, music, dance, and dress children are exposed to a different reality. We know that children are better learners and more engaged when they see themselves in and a part of the history and educational process. There are so many heritage sites that offer direct, in-person story lines to Ghanaian history and the history of Africa. It's important to expose children to history that allows them to see themselves in history beyond being enslaved.

There is an abundance of nature for hands-on agricultural-learning. There are many skilled tradespeople who can help provide internship experiences for students to learn new skills that can spark future entrepreneurial efforts. And where affordable and accessible, trips to neighboring countries allow an expansive opportunity and introduction to more cultural experiences. There are so many non-traditional or formal educational opportunities available to supplant your child's education for what is lacking in their formal experience.

The educational system in Ghana is heavily exam-centered. Students work year-round to test and pass an exam that according to placement ranks them in relation to their classmates more often

Education: Theory & Practice

than how they performed against the subject matter. It's not much different than how we're educated in the US and I believe incorporating these external experiences in your child's education will help provide a much-needed departure from the colonial framework and mindset you may encounter with some educational institutions, teachers, and administrators. So much can be available to the parents willing to unlearn, and accept that the most important actor in a child's education is their parents.

My guest contributor for this chapter is a professional educator for over 20 years, has the personal experience of parenting a child matriculating through the educational system in Ghana, and is working as a founder and administrator of a school in Ghana. She is thoroughly immersed in the educational system in Ghana. Shanna Akosua Magee is a graduate of the University of Massachusetts at Amherst, a Fulbright Scholar, and served as a licensed K-12 School superintendent in Massachusetts.

Introducing Shannan Akosua Magee>>>>>

Repatriates, Expatriates, Transnationals, Binationals, the Black Exodus crew, Pan-Africanists, ADOS, Garveyites, H.U.G.s, Blaxit people; or whatever we call ourselves these days, "all of we" should become familiar with the nuisances of the Ghana education system. The thought of relocating to another country can be super overwhelming. However, having access to good education upon arrival and knowing that your children are straight can reduce relocation anxiety. After all, our children deserve the brightest future we can offer.

It was my son's second trip to Ghana. He made friends easily and he quickly became the newest sensation in Mateheko; a neighborhood near Kaneshie Market in Accra, Ghana. I knew in my heart, that him moving to Ghana at that time was the right thing to do. I had already made up my mind. But getting my son to leave his friends (again), his first love- Sarafina, his way of life, was not going to be easy.

One of the biggest regrets in my life was allowing my 11th grade son to return to the United States to graduate high school. My son, Najja came thru the Nsoromma School, a private Afrikan-centered school tucked away in the Mecca of Black Culture, the West End of Atlanta. Allow me to explain and brag a bit. My son's Principal, the founder, is Dr. Madge Willis known as "Mama Esi". The Jegnas of Nsoromma consisted of Dr. Marimba Ani, Mama Yaa Baruti, Mama Virgie and Baba Morrow (owners of Fruit Veggies and Herbs on Campbelton Road in SW) and the late, great Dr. Asa Hilliard.

My son's Rite of Passage Jegnas were Baba Kweku Densu (now Professor at FAMU), Baba Aiyetoro of the Afrikan Djeli (Master Drummer and Dance Teacher) Baba Yohance Daryll Bediako Mitchell, Baba Kweku & Mama Abena Opare, Mwalimu K. Baruti and Baba Wekesa Madzimoya. Najja's rite of passage process included learning about the Akan and he was eventually initiated at the annual Sankofa Conference held in Washington D.C. While my son was well prepared and ready for Afrika, it seems, I was not.

Having made up my mind, well sort of; I inquired about him attending school through my mentor Dr. Mansah Prah, Professor of Sociology at University of Cape Coast. Along with her two high school aged sons, she had previously visited us in Atlanta. She was very familiar with my expectations and the American system of learning. She patiently took her time to point out the many differences and concerns associated with foreign children attending school in Ghana, especially the traditional hazing of incoming freshmen at high schools and universities. I listened. I wanted to move forward.

Education: Theory & Practice

I contacted Achimota School which was considered one of Ghana's top schools at the time. They had a good reputation for integrating international students. After speaking with school officials, I was told that my son would have to repeat the 10th grade as a condition to enroll because they did not take transfer students. It was their policy for students to start school at the beginning of their curriculum. I wasn't happy about him repeating the 10th grade because I carefully analyzed their curriculum and concluded that the curriculum was corny. Nonetheless, I was still open to the idea of Najja staying in Ghana to learn the language, the culture and the indigenous ways of his people.

But then it happened. My mama, my sister, my aunties, my cousins, and "err body else" had an opinion. None of them had ever traveled to Africa. Their fears ranged from my son having an asthma attack, missing out on his high school prom, getting bit by snakes, eaten by a lion, applying for financial aid for college, missing out on scholarship opportunities, missing out on family reunions, and of course missing out on them calling his name during his high school graduation. Their fears eventually became my own. My voice was overturned and drowned out. In my family, the elders can and do pull rank. So, I listened. I allowed my son to return to Atlanta to graduate high school and unfortunately, the decision still haunts me.

As a parent, school administrator, educator and now Ghanaian citizen, it is my opinion that Ghana has a solid education system. Ghanaian families take education very seriously. The media often portrays otherwise but don't believe the hype. When it comes to education, Ghana has the same problems and lack of resources that plague the rural south across America. Think of it this way, if Ghana's education system was so poor; why are the top American Institutions competing so hard to offer Ghanaian students full scholarships?

Education: Theory & Practice

I remember working at the U.S. Embassy in Ghana where I had the opportunity to meet the President of Indiana University, Michael McRobbie. It was during a dinner meeting at the Movenpick and he insisted that I sit next to him during our meet and greet. I was introducing the Mandela Fellowship Program as part of the Young African Leadership Initiative (now referred to as YALI), a new program that we rolled out during the Obama Administration. Part of my job was to identify Universities that would be interested in hosting African scholars. Well, once I shared the vision of the program, President McRobbie immediately said, "Say no more, I'm in, what do we need to do..". I wasn't all that surprised at his quick commitment of support. Indiana University has been a consistent supporter of African curriculum since the 1970's and has a strong African Studies Program that offers more African languages than any other U.S. college or university. I was only sad that I wasn't sitting at the same table, for the same reason with Presidents of HBCU's. Indiana University had their entire executive team in Ghana; ready to forge new partnerships. The Memorandum of Understanding was signed before he left. So, when I hear that Ghana has a poor education, I know better. I know that all eyes are on Africa.

So now that you've shortlisted Ghana, here are a few things that you should know. First, there is a four-tier education system in Ghana. There are public schools called government schools. These schools are tuition free schools and available in every neighborhood and community. However, expenses for books, uniforms, and feeding are additional. There are semi-private government schools that have hidden entry requirements. These are public schools that "act" private and are usually boarding schools located in Cape Coast, Greater Accra and Kumasi. Normally, you have to know somebody to gain entry; otherwise, the high school entry selection computer system will "randomly" fail you. Graduates of these schools go on to pursue Ivy League schools. The learning environment is very competitive. These

Education: Theory & Practice

schools have a rich long list of Who's Who among their alumni. These institutions have traditionally produced Ghana's ruling class of elites.

Next, there are private schools. These are schools such as East Airport International School, Tema International School (TIS), New Nation School, Ghana Christian High School to name a few. Tuition and fees of these schools start at $2500 or more per term. Most offer payment plans. These schools cater to Ghana's international community and Diasporans. Students who graduate from these schools usually attend university outside of the country including the Ivies. However, post Black Lives Matter and COVID-19 era, there is a growing trend for these students to remain in Ghana. Many Ghanaian parents fear for their children's safety when studying in America due to the increased police brutality and murders of Black people. COVID-19 has deterred Ghanaian students from studying abroad in Asia. I should also mention that within the last five years or so, more Ghanaians are exploring HBCU's as an alternative.

Lastly, there are a few Accra based schools that cater to the very wealthy and diplomatic communities of Ghana, I refer to them as "PRIVATE". They are Ghana International School (GIS), Lincoln School and SOS located in Tema. Tuition and fees begin at $20,000 plus per year. These schools have a diverse teaching staff, a diverse student population and offer higher levels of campus security. Ghanaian students who attend these schools are connected to wealthy families. Diplomats educate their children at these schools and their tuition and fees are usually subsidized by governments and multinational companies. These students go on to Ivy Leagues, assume ownership of family businesses, receive executive jobs at multinational companies, or simply chill. Interestingly enough, these schools have reserved slots at Ivy Leagues in America. For example, students at GIS brag openly

Education: Theory & Practice

about how their Class Presidents are traditionally offered admission with full rides at an Ivy League school.

For parents considering relocation to Ghana and searching for schools K-12; allow me to help you save some energy. Unless you are married into a Ghanaian family or believe you can move mountains, I encourage you to select a private school for several reasons. First, private schools will allow you to have more input in your children's education on a day-to-day basis and offer better customer service. While there are some excellent government schools, most lack the view that they are in partnership with parents.

Secondly, choosing a government school for your child is almost like giving away your autonomous right to make decisions for your child's education. This can be a good thing if you buy into the notion that it takes a village to raise a child. However, government schools are usually "conveyer belt" minded and lack the instructional support and resources needed to cater to each child's unique talents and produce critical thinkers. These schools come with rote instruction with excessive, needless bureaucracy and will only frustrate you. There is however, a bright side. I am optimistic, as more and more Diasporan return to Ghana and gain leadership roles in education; improvements will be made.

Another reason to consider funding a private education is because government schools are usually conservative and follow rigid protocols. Keep in mind, Ghana still has corporal punishment. Student discipline is a very serious matter and teachers will 'lay hands' on students. In fact, Ghanaian Diasporan send their children back to Ghana because of the strict discipline. As a former high school principal in Ghana, I have observed Ghanaian parents who live in Europe tricking their children to visit Ghana for summer vacations and then leave them behind. These students start off being angry but ultimately, they come around. When it's time for them to go back to London or the U.K., the children lose interest.

Education: Theory & Practice

Over the years, several Ghanaian parents have personally thanked me for helping their teenagers make adjustments.

There are many examples of government schools following "nonsensical" protocols. In 2021, you can find government schools in Ghana banning African children from receiving an education because they wear African hair. The most recent case was largely publicized when a Rastafarian student was banned and asked to cut his hair as a requirement to attend school despite his impeccable record of student achievement. The same government school, Achimota - also called "Motown" by Ghanaians - did not require white and mixed-race international students to cut their hair to receive an education. This issue quickly became "WhatsApp forward chat" around the globe.

In a world where we are desperately trying to teach our youth to celebrate their natural selves; this is a problem. I do not want any repatriate to find themselves in such a battle with school authorities. How can we relocate to Africa to battle identity politics? This is nonsense. However, again, I am optimistic that with the return of so many Diasporans integrating into school leadership, I see these protocols fading away.

Having a successful experience of integrating your children into formal education in Ghana largely depends on their age, grade level, and your network. It can be challenging to transfer into a government school after primary (elementary) school. If you enroll your child in first grade or P1 (Primary one) in Ghana, most government schools will admit them with little to no questions asked. One of the reasons this becomes more difficult in middle school is because students are heavily tracked due to the Basic Education Certificate Examination (BECE). All ninth graders will take the BECE exam to enter high school. In addition, this exam pretty much dictates if your child will study the Arts or Sciences at the University level. Once a child reaches high school level, the game changes.

Education: Theory & Practice

If your child does not perform well in their science courses on the BECE exam; some unknown, random, decision maker will decide your child can no longer be a nurse, doctor, physical therapist, or engineer. Unlike in American middle schools, most students usually take a state mandated skills-based exam. While these results may impact overall local school performance and ultimately property values, these scores hardly determine which career path students pursue or which courses students can take in high school. An exception to this norm may be students that need prerequisite classes or scores to pursue Gifted, Honors or AP classes in high school.

When searching for schools, keep in mind that most government high schools are residential schools and are single gender . However, post COVID-19 era, many of these schools are now offering day options for students. Most private schools are co-ed and almost all, offer day school or residential options. Ghana is legally Anti-LGBTQ and Ghanaians in general, are not open to any gender fluid conversations. So, for now, don't even try it.

Private school educators usually have some pre-disposition to differing global ideologies and exposure to other cultures and societies. These environments appear to be more tolerant and open to diversity.

There are several schools in Ghana that offer specialized learning plans for students with learning disabilities be them physical, mental or emotional. Currently, it is difficult to get necessary assessments and psychological evaluations for children. I highly recommend getting such evaluations with learning plans done prior to relocating to Ghana. Once you have the learning plans in hand, most schools can implement them provided they do not require any sophisticated technology.

I have both a niece and a nephew that are autistic. My nephew, Kayvon is low functioning autistic and my niece Kiki is high

Education: Theory & Practice

functioning - gifted. Educating Kiki would be a lot easier and cheaper than educating Kayvon in Ghana. While both are autistic; their needs are extremely different. Kiki only needed a speech pathologist for a few months in elementary school. Kayvon will need help with speech during his adult life. Finding a speech pathologist in Ghana is rare. In addition, children with special needs may require frequent specialized assessments. Private schools that specialized in teaching children with Autism can offer tuition and fees that begin at $5,000 per term. Special Education Instructors are needed in Ghana. However, most schools cannot afford to pay special education teacher salaries. #ijs

Unlike in America where most schools operate on a quarterly basis; Ghanaian private schools operate on trimesters. Hence, there are three terms you must pay for. Most schools offer a discount if you were to pay all fees upfront. However, if a school fails to mention any discount; don't hesitate to ask. In fact, I encourage it. Most private schools offer discounted rates when you enroll multiple children from one family (cousins included). If you have teaching experience, you can sometimes barter employment for discounted tuition. Ask if you can work or teach part time at your child's school to reduce tuition. Principals at private schools have more flexibility to offer such arrangements and may welcome the strength. The best way for you to learn more about the expectations of the school is to attend the parent teacher association (PTA) executive meetings. Take advantage and learn about the Executive Members of the Board. Your school's PTA can often serve as a networking machine. PTA's in Ghana have a lot of power.

Please keep in mind that private schools charge tuition and fees but there are usually no internal financial aid or grants to subsidize the costs. These schools are typically owned by a family and rely heavily on tuition & fees to run the day-to-day operations of the institution. What is meant by tuition and fees? Tuition is usually

Education: Theory & Practice

the cost of attending the school. Fees are all the other costs such as: Uniforms, feeding (3 meals per day), sports or athletics fees, excursion fees (field trips), teacher gifts year-round, and of course EXTRA CLASSES.

When purchasing uniforms, there are about three uniforms for sale. One is a traditional uniform, the other is a variation, and the third is an athletic uniform. Most schools in Ghana are very strict about uniform compliance. This includes the socks, shoes, hairstyles, jewelry, etc. Hairstyles should not be a problem at a private school. Most private schools tend to be flexible, however, do your due diligence and check to see if your school allows children to wear braids, extensions, and or locs.

In Ghana, if your child is learning, making good grades, and you are satisfied; it is usual to dash (tip) the teacher or buy nice gifts at Xmas. Since its part of Ghanaian culture to give and receive gifts, I always pick days like Malcolm X's birthday, or Juneteenth to thank my fellow teachers and tutors. I used to make Kwanzaa gifts for my staff. This was one method of me sharing my culture with the staff and setting the stage for me to provide greater insight of Black History with my Ghanaian colleagues. Your children can also do this in their classrooms.

However, if your child is struggling, it is very common to ask teachers to perform private tutorial classes after school. (In America, this is against the law in most school districts; teachers are not allowed to take payments for afterschool or weekend tutoring for students they teach during the school day.) Tutors range from $5-$10 an hour. However, just barter by the month with the tutor. Select specific hours on the weekends in your home. Be sure to include "deductions" in the bargaining. If tutors do not show up on time or as schedule, you can deduct some amount.

I remember hiring a Brown University 3rd year student for a tutor. She was studying abroad in Ghana. I needed her to work with my son in Chemistry. We were on vacation in Ghana and I needed to stay longer beyond the two weeks school vacation. So, I arranged homeschool classes with his school district in Georgia so he could receive high school credits for Chemistry. It basically consisted of me keeping track of his hours of instruction and faxing his schedule and his assignments. So even if you are on a long-term vacation in Africa and sorting out your relocation move, try to schedule extra tutoring in math or science for the children. This could also be supplemental instruction such as yoga, dance class, star gazing, or gardening as well. I don't believe in children being idle.

The learning curriculum in Ghana is suspect but so are American school curriculums. Don't be surprised when your child learns about a White Jesus in African schools. Beyond the bombardment of White Jesus Images on Tro Tros and billboards in Ghana, White Jesus is part of the school curriculum. Ghanaian students take a course call RME (Religious and Moral Education). Pick up any RME Pupil textbook and read it yourself. If you find it okay, then no problem. But if you find fault, you may have to teach your child how to discriminate between what is being taught at school and his or her own family values. This is similar to teaching your child good eating habits. If you are a Vegan, you teach your child what to eat and what not to eat.

My sister's kids overdosed on reading labels. My nephew Jahkobee would come to my house and read everything-expiration dates, ingredients, and basically give you a research presentation on the ingredients and why he was or was not going to eat something. My other nephews, Judah, Israel, and Zion were much better. They learned to discriminate between eating Doritos nachos and ingredients such as Red 40. If you teach your children who they are before they leave the house, this course will not be a problem for them. If your children leave your house and begin to worship White Gods, I can only assume it's because you want them to have a worldview perspective. Fair enough!

Education: Theory & Practice

Again, much like the American school system, you will have to de-program your child on most of what they will learn. But here is the good part about the Ghanaian curriculum: Science and Mathematics...you can't beat it. In American schools you will not learn about Agriculture infused in Science. In Ghana, your children will learn how to grow food as a part of the curriculum.

In closing, I have tried to provide a few critical factors to consider when researching schools in Ghana. When leaving America or the Western society including the Caribbean, your child will gain so much more by receiving an education in a safe, loving and nurturing environment. Though some schools in Ghana lack resources and technology infrastructure; schools in Ghana do not lack a loving staff. Government schools, private schools, and PRIVATE schools encourage and inspire students to learn. Overall, teachers in Ghana work hard and bring good energy and love for children to the classroom-a missing ingredient in Western education. Your child will go from hating to do homework to doing homework all the time. Your child's natural curiosity will grow and his or her conversations and discussions at home begin to change. Children of repatriates have a lot to offer to the learning environments in Ghana.. Their stories, histories, and travel experiences are needed to improve the Ghanaian Education System. Our children by default, provide rich content and context for Ghanaian children to better understand the concept of the MAAFA. This is how we bridge the Gap. We culturally immerse ourselves into Afrikan culture to dispel the negative stereotypes about Africa and demystify her. Remember, the only purpose of a formal education is to liberate ourselves from bondage and free the land! Here are a few tips to help you get started. Good Luck!

Disclosure: For the purpose of this article, I am biased toward high schools since they are the most difficult to navigate in Ghana. Grades K-9 have straight forward, transparent enrollment requirements.

Education: Theory & Practice

If you are looking for a Kindergarten, referred to as KG, look for one in your neighborhood close to your home. The teacher or instructor should have a decent command over English. Your child has to be able to communicate what happened in school every day.

If you are looking for an elementary school, look for one in your neighborhood. This will save you on both money and time. Traffic is out of control. The curriculum is the same. Do not pay attention to Montessori Marketing. Most schools in Ghana are not Montessori accredited. Look for schools that are neat, have staff that use technology, and have a Principal that returns phone calls and communicates with parents. Also, ask the Principal about extracurricular activities.

If you are looking for a middle school, look for one in your neighborhood. Pay for extra tutorials. One on one tutoring is recommended to help middle school students achieve mastery across the subjects. This way if there are any gaps in your child's understanding, it can be addressed. Also, look for a school that offer extracurricular activities.

If you are looking for a high school- I recommend immersing your child in the culture which means a boarding school. However, if you think your child cannot recover from the culture shock, select a good school with a day school option. The friends your teenager will make in Ghana at boarding school tend to become lifetime friends and their business network later in life.

University- Attending University in Ghana is inexpensive and doable. I recommend attending one of Ghana's flagship schools such as UG (University of Ghana), UCC (University of Cape Coast) or Tech (known as Kwame Nkrumah University of Science & Technology) or anyone of the top Private Universities for newer programs such as: Ashesi University, Academic City University College, or Webster college. A bachelor's degree from a private university range anywhere from $5,000 plus. An engineering

Education: Theory & Practice

degree from a private quality university in Ghana can cost less than $16,000. Do not send your children back to America to accumulate loans. Universities in Ghana are now beginning to offer Diasporan students, special consideration and scholarships. Grow your children to be debt free so they may continue to build your family Legacy.

Note: Though you may find a perfect school; you will have to consider where you live and the time the children spend traveling to school. If it takes more than 30 minutes for your child to get to school, then it's too far. No matter what, we as parents homeschool by default. With that said, do not rob your child of a true, authentic Afrikan experienced by choosing to "homeschool". Allow him or her to gain genuine, first-hand authentic Afrikan experiences among children in Ghana.

Recommendations for Schools (K-12): Airport Residential, Haatso, Adenta, East Legon, Roman Ridge, Cantonments, Labone, West Legon, North Legon, Kwabenya, East Legon Hills, Ashale Botwye, Adjiringanor, Aburi, Kumasi, Konongo, Tamale, Atimpoku, Cape Coast, Tema

Education: Theory & Practice

Donate Books for our Library
or we can help you build your own

MANAGING YOUR PRIVILEGE, EXPECTATIONS & RELATIONSHIPS

Managing your privilege, expectations and relationships is more difficult if you're doing it alone. I would highly suggest repatriating in teams, small groups or a family who serve as each other's accountability partners.

Privilege

Privilege is everywhere. If you're reading this book with the serious thought and plan to move to Africa, the truth of the matter is that you have some level of privilege that will allow you to pack up and move to another country. The fact that you're able to consider moving – let alone to another country - and can afford it is privilege. The fact that you're a United States citizen, despite the craziness we go through as people of African descent, comes with a certain level of privilege itself.

This is not necessarily negative or counter-productive. It means the generations before made a way for things to be easier for us to have the benefit of some privilege. I don't think the idea of privilege is a problem or challenge vs the application of said privilege. And I don't think you have to become a full blown socialist to appreciate and apply your privilege positively.

<<<<<<<<Let's Talk about Privilege in Ghana

Because we live in what seems to be shaping up as a complete cancel culture right now, the basic idea of privilege is wrapped in majority negative connotations. We often call out white privilege, male privilege and wealthy privilege – rightfully so. Social media – especially the absolute hilarious Black Twitter - has so many people denouncing

Managing Your Privilege, Expectations & Relationships

or trying to shed their privilege instead of using it to create some balance and equity.

Managing your privilege starts with an acknowledgement of the fact that you have some privilege. I acknowledge my privilege. I also acknowledge the enormous sacrifices that have been made for me to enjoy my privilege. My privilege comes from hundreds of years of hard work, fighting for basic freedoms and sacrifices to ensure I could have the privilege of a decent education, opportunity, and a decolonized mind and spirit. I acknowledge the amount of work that has been poured into me directly and indirectly so that my primary application of privilege is to help others. And you can't help others if you're struggling to help to yourself.

If you're considering moving to Ghana from the US, you're moving to a country where the dollar has been historically strong allowing Diasporans to have an economically favorable advantage. Although Ghana can be very expensive and the real life value of the dollar will fluctuate. So there's an economic privilege you will possess in some instances.

I am not a judge or member of a jury so I am not telling you what to do, but if you're interested in not being a jerk, remaining sensitive to the fact that there are acute cultural differences and that it takes a conscious mind to work in, with, and alongside a new community of people, then you will want to check your privilege.

There are historical divides and misconceptions between us as Africans in the diaspora – especially African Americans – and continental Africans. This divide was created by the same colonizers who kidnapped us, brainwashed us, and continue to perpetuate a fabricated conflict that aims to prevent us from realizing we are the same people and loving up on one another because they know our power and are afraid of it. It's the same power that birthed human civilization as we know it. If you're looking to build African unity, being extra careful and taking extra

Managing Your Privilege, Expectations & Relationships

steps such as paying attention to how you exercise your privilege is underrated and extremely important.

While there may not be systemic racism in Ghana, there is classism and tribalism. Just as Black people lost their identity, the brothers and sisters on the continent lost us (many of whom were considered to be half of the strongest, brightest and most resilient to endure the torture of chattel slavery) and were oppressed under colonial rule.

Many buckled under pressure and began to help the colonizers to save themselves from suffering. We are literally opposite sides of the colonization coin. So unless we're having a who is the most oppressed contest, let's be cognizant of what and how we bring ourselves. Let's bring the best of ourselves.

We definitely have to stop thinking of the African continent and African people as poor. Everybody in Africa is not looking for you to sponsor them with a green card even though sometimes it may feel like it. Africa is the richest land mass on the planet. But poverty is very real.

Those of us who have repatriated may not like to mention it and speak frankly because they haven't acknowledged their privilege, but many of us have moved here because of the economic advantage. You can have a nanny, driver, house help, butler and gardener on staff monthly for the price of a Michelin star dinner at the chef's table for one night. NO CAP!

I'm not judging. It's just a fact. Most of us who repatriate didn't come from wealthy families. We don't come from generational wealth. We watched our parents and grandparents struggle. We struggled through high school and college. We worked hard to get in, graduate and get a great job or start our business. We've made a certain number of personal sacrifices where we feel we deserve a certain lifestyle and we will go wherever we can get it.

These jobs have to be done and more than you may know it, you're providing income that's more than likely supporting more people than you imagine. But it's important to acknowledge that privilege. And it's important to apply it with love, care and intention. That means even though you are employing people, it is your duty to treat people with respect, love and care at a bare minimum. If you are not, you are a Black colonizer and part of the problem. This not only includes how you treat people you employ but how you treat people in the market, when you go out to eat and in general as you move and live about the country.

Expectations

Managing your expectations is imperative for relocation, repatriation, and integration. Your number one benefit will be patience. Unpack your patience now. You will find plenty of inefficiency, unreliability, laziness, greediness and pure nonsense. Everybody isn't out to get you and some people are. Everybody doesn't want a green card, and some people do. A lot of people will say Akwaaba (Welcome) and some don't mean it. A lot of people will call you brother and sister to get close to you and some do so they can steal.

While Africa and Africans are not all poor, poverty is real in Ghana and many African countries. As of 2020, the daily minimum wage in Ghana stood at 11.82 Ghanaian cedis (GHS) (approximately 2.03 U.S. dollars), representing an increase of 1.17 GHS (around 0.2 U.S. dollars) from 2019. Many Ghanaians are overworked and underpaid. The reality is that money is hard to come by and there are people looking for victims. You can expect a lot of people to solicit a tip – sometimes for doing no more than their job and sometimes for doing nothing – just because they assume that as an American, you have it to give.

Managing Your Privilege, Expectations & Relationships

Social media photos from Black celebrities and influencers often capture the upside of Accra, the capital city and other larger more developed cities yet rarely go into the country and show the conditions of the majority of the people. I understand the importance of capturing the beauty and magnificent development of Ghana to combat traditional poverty stereotypes but we should not lose focus of the fact that poverty is real.

Let's talk about Expectations in Ghana>>>>>

Some people, no matter what you do or how much you try to help them, will mismanage their life and never get out of poverty. Alcoholism is real. Teenage pregnancy is real. Rape is real. Divorce is real. Family battles are real. Survival is real. Disease is real. The hustle is real. Stupidity is real. Jealously is real. Con artists are real. Ghanaians introduced me to a term called Ghanaian PhD which stands for pull him down. Unfortunately, it feels like too many people want to sabotage, steal ideas and invest more into cheating you than they do their business. As you move around and begin to meet more people you will find that some Ghanaians have a general distrust of other Ghanaians. Sound familiar? It doesn't take long to experience it and it can confuse you and throw you off at first. It's interesting and important not to allow the few to color your entire experience or characterizations of all Ghanaians.

It will be important to figure out how to balance your emotional attachment to "being home". This will help you to navigate your less than favorable experiences. It's important to readjust your idea of what you think about Africa. Don't get me wrong. You can still lead with love. You can still have an open heart and you must keep an open mind. And you don't and shouldn't come with a chip on your shoulder or expect to be cheated. But you should deal with people according to how they deal with you.

Managing Your Privilege, Expectations & Relationships

Many of us who made the transition are partially responsible for not taking the time to do our best and paint an accurate picture for you for fear we may discourage you. We have this romantic idea, which is understandable, of returning to the motherland, kissing the ground and sinking our feet in the dirt. But there are very real experiences and flags that should not be ignored. And since we are talking about real, boots-on-the-ground, nationbuilding, not media illusions, it can really be a matter of life or death.

Prior to coming and spending a serious amount of time on the ground in Ghana, I was fairly clear that continental African complicity in the trans-Atlantic slave trade was grossly overstated and another ploy by colonizers to further divide us. After spending the time I have in Ghana, I am sure that continental African complicity was indeed a cornerstone to the trans-Atlantic slave trade. I'm sure I've met people who inherited their ancestors' treason. This is a conversation I believe we should not shy away from and is necessary for our collective healing. My good friend and publicist, Muhammida recently shared an explanation that offered me a different perspective. She compared it to crack in the 80's. There was so much money flowing around and it seemed like everyone wanted a piece and many were willing to do anything, including selling crack to their own mother and sometimes children. I believe you can equate selling crack to your family to helping colonizers sell us Africans into slavery.

Those of us who grew up in, or adjacent to, any ghetto or project in the U.S., attended urban schools, had a neighborhood drug dealer or used to be the neighborhood drug dealer have been conditioned. We know there are written rules and codes but the most important are often those unwritten and unspoken. So we move with different level of alertness and observation. When you know, you know.

It is extremely important for me to lead into this next point with the fact that Ghana is a relatively new nation. Our expectations of

Managing Your Privilege, Expectations & Relationships

widespread standards of customer service can be simply unrealistic in a place where tourism is a fairly new industry. Customer service standards in most of Ghana's government people facing services and private institutions are non-existent as we know it. We operate from what we feel is logical. A customer has money to spend on a product or service. A business is selling product or the government is fulfilling their duty to offer a service. A business wants the customer to patronize, so the business makes an effort to provide service or product with a high level of care which can mean repeat business. In Ghana, it often feels like the opposite and government and private businesses are willing to leave it to chance. They have the product or service and if you want or need it, then you can deal with their service or take your chances somewhere else. That's the only explanation I can give you because some things are ridiculous and will leave you stunned. Bring a bottle of water and sip patience slowly.

Excellent customer service is hard to come by and it will cost you There are many places with good and great customer service according to international standards but they often come at a different price point. And there are a lot of people in Ghana - diasporan and Ghanaians - who want and appreciate good customer service. Unfortunately, many of the vendors and venues with poor customer service are Ghanaian-owned and many with the better customer service are foreign-owned. I've found all too often that the remedy for poor service is to apologize profusely over and over again, as opposed to changing the behavior. In the end it points to lack of education, training, standards and a competitive marketplace.

Again, pack your patience. Time just doesn't seem to be that important. Late is normal. And not 15 - 20 minutes late but sometimes an hour late or people just not showing up. These are indicators and flags to pay attention to as you're trying to get things done and set up. Sometimes you won't have a choice with certain functions and you just have to deal with it. For example, traffic is a big inhibitor so learning the traffic patterns will help. But sometimes people are just late. If you think CPT (Colored People's Time) is bad just know it's hereditary. APT (African People's Time) is much worse so at least we've gotten better over time. In general everything may seem to take a little longer and streamlined processes will seem like they don't exist.

The beauty in all of this critique and every gap I've mentioned is that there is such an enormous opportunity for the right person with grit, patience, resilience and a serious commitment to see change through, to do very well for themselves and help make a necessary change for the country at the same time. It will take just as much if not more patience and management of your expectations to see the opportunity through. So again - pack your patience and manage your expectations.

You should also note that even with everything that may read harsh or hard, I and so many others are still choosing Ghana. We are willing to deal with the areas of improvement because we know freedom ain't free and there's definitely a high level of freedom in Ghana. We're all a bit crazy and we enjoy this battle for freedom because we're fighting to improve our lives and the lives of those around us instead of fighting for acceptance, acknowledgement or begging the police to stop killing us.

Relationships

You have to understand that relationships cannot be underestimated - especially in Ghana. We all know the saying it's not *what* you know, but *who* you know. In Ghana, it's exponentially important. Ghana is steeped in a culture where family, school mates and tribal relationships have ruled both formally and informally for centuries. Relationships are woven into the fabric of everyday life. I would say in my experience, without a doubt, relationships are the most valuable currency you can possess in

Managing Your Privilege, Expectations & Relationships

Ghana. Having the right relationships will help you maneuver your way through the minutia and help you access the services and/or products you need. Repatriating to Ghana is not for the faint of heart. Life can truly be survival of the fittest and connected.

Relationships can make the difference between sitting in line and waiting for hours versus sending a WhatsApp message without wasting time. The difference between getting a seat at a table at the restaurant of your choice versus having to wait a week. The difference between finding that hard to get product at a reasonable price vs. not at all or overpriced. The difference between finding a reputable plumber, electrician, general contractor, painter, etc. vs. a non-reliable worker which will definitely cost you more in cash and time. And most importantly, the right relationship will help you avoid paying what we call the accent tax, which is an escalated price because of your foreign accent.

It's also very important as you begin to make your way through Ghana, meet people, and begin to establish relationships that you make sure you know who you are and you're rooted. What is your relationship with yourself? Going back to mastering your why you also need to master your Who. Who are you? Ghana is like a magical wonderland. There are people from all walks of life and everybody is somebody. Everybody is a prince, princess, king, queen, chief, queen mother or at least one person removed. And they're normally telling the truth but don't let that blind you to your own royalty.

You'll realize that you can be whoever you tell people you are but eventually you'll have to meet yourself one-on-one and it's important not to be confused at the meeting with yourself. Know who you are and get comfortable in your skin. Whether you're wearing struggle or success, be comfortable with it and don't be afraid to be who you are. Once you know who you are, it makes it that easier to find your tribe.

Managing Your Privilege, Expectations & Relationships

It's important not to create or enter a relationship just to get leverage or access to something. Reciprocity is expected and unspoken — it's just how things work. Inauthenticity is a troublesome mask to wear every day and it'll melt in the heat. There are some things you are going to need to go through to have the experience and sharpen your wit. You don't want to cheat yourself. You need to have some stories and lessons of your own to share. You need to meet and have some connections on your own.

Don't put the transaction before the relationship. Actually get to know people and take your time. As you meet people who are connected and they see you as a kindred spirit based on your authenticity, then you meet on even ground. Be patient. Earn your keep and allow things to move smoothly. It takes time. And have something to offer — a resource, perspective, art, idea or just a strong unwavering voice willing to stand for something.

<<<<<Let's talk about Relationships in Ghana

There are so many people in Ghana on their hustle. Ghanaians and expats fighting for their dream, looking for a deal, creating a start-up, or trying to get a government contract. So many looking to be a big man or big woman, get invited to the big wedding, get invited to the private socialite birthday party, gain access to hottest WhatsApp Groups and have people know their name. It's important for you to stay grounded or you can get swept up in the popularity tsunami.

There are various diaspora communities in Ghana you will have an opportunity to experience. I am happy I figured it out early and didn't align myself with any one group over another. Aunties and uncles who moved to Ghana from the States and Caribbean 15 - 30 years ago, made a life and have been here to see Ghana change overtime. US Embassy, USAID, military and NGO

Managing Your Privilege, Expectations & Relationships

employees who live in Ghana on assignments and have chosen Africa as their preference for assignments. Pan-African revolutionaries, government contractors and importers/exporters. Young professionals. Rasta community. Members of the Pan Hellenic Council (Black Greek letter organizations). RQQ to the Bruhs. Traditionalists. Young Ghanaian Diasporans who were born and/or schooled in the states and decided to come back home. Ghana/UK Crew.

When I first started travelling back and forth to Ghana, I had this idea that I would find this utopian unified group of Black people living in a community with this ideal cooperative system of living and working together without the in-fighting that I see in the States within many "enlightened" Black communities. I was wrong. We are all humans from different backgrounds with different personalities and different perspectives. More often than not, we are all jockeying for the same position in the same space.

I will always be about people who want to work together towards a common goal and when that can't happen, it's ok to wish folks well and keep it moving. It's ok to attend meetings, support where you can, speak when you see people and leave it where its is without the need for a follow up conversation or meeting. Don't expect all Black people to get along because you're in Africa together.

Again, there exists an opportunity for someone or some people in this gap. I've always felt that we needed a Black census and annual report in Ghana detailing our African American population in Ghana.

Although I've travelled and spent the majority of my time in Ghana by myself, meaning without my family and close friends at home, I'm on daily chats with my bros, my family, my wife and my children. And I have lots of friends and family who come often and travel back and forth so I am able to manage pretty well. And I have Nyame Bekyere.

Managing Your Privilege, Expectations & Relationships

Knowing yourself is important because no matter how many people you meet, become close with and actually establish real friendships, it gets lonely at times and it's nothing like family and friends who you've been rocking with all your life. As you consider your move and plan for success, remember to manage yourself well. You don't want Ghana to manage you. Take a moment to think about this chapter and use the next few pages to explore your own ideas about privilege and how you apply yours; your expectations; how you deal with disappointments; and what core values are non-negotiable in your relationships.

Here's a reading list on Privilege, Expectations and Relationships>>>>>>>>>>

HONORABLE & YOU: THE GOVERNMENT

It's important to keep in mind you're considering moving to a country where many of the indigenous people want out and have sometimes very different opinions of the government – just as we have about America. As much as many of us in the Diaspora are interested in moving to Ghana to either get away from the racism and injustice or because of what we see as opportunities, many citizens have legitimate concerns about what they want to see from their own government.

Citizens have their own political party affiliation and often feel very strongly about it. It's important to respect this fact and do your own research before you pick a side. Ghanaians are serious about their political affiliation and every party has their perspective on what and who is the best for Ghana. You should definitely follow Ghana Twitter and do some deeps dives in you're interested in getting involved in government relations.

I personally don't get involved in politics. It's not my wheelhouse. I have always been an independent registered voter in Washington, DC and I don't see myself changing anytime soon. I have my own questions and reservations about western political structures and the effectiveness of democratic governance models and operations.. I am grateful to Ghana's current government led by Nana Addo Dankwa Akufo Addo. I've had the opportunity to work closely with him and his administration on the Year of Return and am adjacently involved with Beyond the Return. As a public administrator by training, entrepreneur by choice, and community development advocate by divine intervention, I live at the intersection of government, business and community service to find alignment on the three different bottom lines.

If you're repatriating to Ghana, you need to have a general understanding of how the government works and is set up. You

Honorable & You: The Government

need a basic understanding of where Ghana sits in the world marketplace and how it functions with its delicate composition of traditional and democratic authorities. Everything will not make sense immediately but as you make the final move and have various experiences on the ground, having an understanding of the history of the government and how it works technically will help you understand your place in it all. It will also aid in building relationships with people you meet and most importantly, begin to learn more about Ghana. If you plan on doing business, especially big business or making significant investments, I underscore paying attention and minding your business.

We're going to do two things in this chapter: (1) provide you with a comprehensive overview of the government's political structure and functions; and (2) our guest contributor, Danny Damah, will discuss government programs from an investment/business perspective focusing on industrial and social investment opportunities from a government public/private partnership to help us understand from his experiences and knowledge where Ghana is going, how you fit in, and some general nuggets that will help you as you interact.

Read the Ghanaian Constitution>>>>>>>

The Ghanaian political hierarchal power structure is as follows:

1. President
2. Vice President
3. Speaker of Parliament
4. Chief Justice
5. Ministers
6. Parliamentarians
7. Municipal Chief Executives
8. Presiding Members
9. Assembly Members

Honorable & You: The Government

Elections in Ghana are conducted every four years as instructed by the 1992 Constitution of Ghana. The 1992 constitution provides the basic charter for the fourth attempt at a democratic government since independence in 1957. Drawn up with the intent of preventing future coups, dictatorial government, and one party states, it is said to be designed to foster tolerance and the concept of power-sharing models. Much of it was drawn from US democracy and governance structure.

The constitution provides for the sharing of powers among a president, a parliament, a cabinet, a Council of State, and an independent judiciary. Executive authority is shared by the president, the twenty-five member Council of State, and numerous advisory bodies, including the National Security Council. The president is head of state, head of government, and commander in chief of the armed forces of Ghana. He also appoints the vice president.

The president is elected for a four-year term by the people. The Parliament of Ghana has 275 members, elected for a four-year term in single-seat constituencies. The presidential election is won by having more than 50% of valid votes cast. The voting system is a two-party system, namely New Patriotic Party (NPP)- the current ruling party and the National Democratic Congress (NDC). Elections have been held every four years since 1992 with Presidential and parliamentary elections held alongside each other generally on December 7th every four years.

Kwame Nkrumah, who was the incumbent Prime Minister and leader of the Convention People's Party (CPP) defeated J. B. Danquah, leader of the United Party in Ghana's first election held on April 27, 1960. Ghana became a republic, with Kwame Nkrumah as President. Due to the peoples overwhelming support of him Ghana became a one-party state in 1964 with, the CPP being the sole authorized party. However, less than a year later, Nkrumah was removed by military coup which was the first of four coups.

The subsequent coups came in 1972, 1979, and 1981. From December 1981 until November 1992 Ghana was ruled by a Provisional National Defence Council (PNDC). Ghana has held relatively peaceful elections since the 1992 election and constitution. An interesting fact is that up through this past election in December 2020, the US and Ghana had identical party elections. Every time the republican party won, NPP won; and every time the Democratic party won, NDC won.

Ghana has a unicameral legislature composed of 275 Members of Parliament who come from single-member constituencies. The President appoints Ministers of whom the majority, by rule of the Constitution, have to come from Parliament. A minister is a politician who heads a ministry, making and implementing decisions on policies in conjunction with the other ministers to help the President fill his mandate. His Excellency Nana Addo, Ghana's current President, selected 46 Ministers for his second term of which 30 form the central government and 16 form the regional government authorities.

Central Government
1. Minister Of National Security – Albert Kan Dapaah
2. Minister Of Finance – Ken Ofori-Atta
3. Minister Of Trade And Industry – Alan Kyerematen
4. Minister Of Defence – Hon. Dominic Nitiwul, MP
5. Minister Of Interior – Hon. Ambrose Dery, MP
6. Minister Of Foreign Affairs And Regional Integration – Shirley Ayorkor Botchwey
7. Minister Of Attorney General And Minister For Justice – Godfred Dame
8. Minister Of Local Government, Decentralization And Rural Development – Hon. Dan Botwe, MP
9. Minister Of Parliamentary Affairs – Hon. Osei Kyei Mensah Bonsu, MP

10. Minister Of Communication And Digitization – Hon. Ursula Owusu-Ekuful, MP
11. Minister Of Food And Agriculture – Dr. Owusu Afriyie Akoto
12. Minister Of Energy – Hon. Dr. Matthew Opoku Prempeh, MP
13. Minister Of Education – Hon. Dr. Yaw Osei Adutwum, MP
14. Minister Of Health – Hon. Kwaku Agyemang Manu, MP
15. Minister Of Lands And Natural Resources – Hon. Samuel Abdulai Jinapor, MP
16. Minister Of Roads And Highways – Kwasi Amoako Atta, MP
17. Minister Of Works And Housing – Hon. Francis Asenso Boakye, MP
18. Minister Of Transport – Kwaku Ofori Asiamah
19. Minister Of Fisheries And Aquaculture Development – Hon. Mavis Hawa Koomson, MP
20. Minister Of Railway Development – Hon. John Peter Amewu, MP
21. Minister Of Sanitation And Water Resources – Cecilia Abena Dapaah
22. Minister Of Tourism, Art And Culture – Awal Mohammed
23. Minister Of Gender, Children And Social Protection – Hon. Sarah Adwoa safo, MP
24. Minister Of Chieftaincy And Religious Affairs – Hon. Ebenezer Kojo Kum, MP
25. Minister Of Environment, Science, Technology And Innovation – Hon. Dr. Kwaku Afriyie, MP
26. Minister Of Employment And Labour Relations – Hon. Ignatius Baffuor Awuah, MP
27. Minister Of Information – Hon. Kojo Oppong Nkrumah, MP
28. Minister Of Youth And Sports – Hon. Mustapha Yussif, MP
29. Minister Of Public Enterprises – Hon. Joseph Cudjoe, MP
30. Minister Of Works and Housing (Minister Of State) – Hon. Freda Prempeh, MP

Regional Government

1. Ahafo Region – George Boakye
2. Ashanti Region – Simon Osei-Mensah
3. Bono Region – Justina Owusu-Banahene
4. Bono East Region – Adu Gyan
5. Central Region – Justina Marigold Assan
6. Eastern Region – Seth Acheampong
7. Greater Accra Region – Hon. Henry Quartey, MP
8. Northern Region – Shani Alhassan Saibu
9. North East Region – Yidana Zakaria
10. Otis Region – Joseph Makubu

Honorable & You: The Government

11. Savanna Region – Saeed Muhazu Jibril
12. Upper East Region – Stepen Yakubu
13. Upper West Region – Dr. Hafiz Bin Salih
14. Volta Region – Dr. Archibald Yao Letsa
15. Western Region – Hon. Kwabena Okyere Darko Mensah, MP
16. Western North Region – Richard Obeng

Ghana's Parliament▷>>>>>>>>>>>>

A term of the Parliament of Ghana spans over a period of four (4) years with each year comprising a session of not more than 12 months. During sessions of Parliament there are periods of Meetings and Sittings. By Constitutional law, the Speaker of Parliament exercises the power of summoning a new Session of Parliament. In practice, the first Session of Parliament begins on the 7th of January approximately a month after the general election.

On average, Parliament sits for 28 weeks and goes on recess for 24 weeks within a session. The House sits from Tuesday to Friday, making an average of 132 sittings in a session. All parliamentary proceedings happen at the Parliament House in Accra. Ordinarily, there are three meetings in a session: (1) 1st meeting is January to March; 2nd meeting is May to July and the 3rd meeting is October to December. As a Member of Parliament their primary duty is scrutinizing statutory instruments and voting to pass bills into law.

The Ghanaian Judiciary branch is divided into two sections: the Superior Courts of the Judicature, and lower level courts or tribunals. The Superior Courts of Judicature as dictated by the constitution are the Supreme Court, the Court of Appeal, and the High Court and Regional Tribunals. The lower level courts and tribunals are established on a case-by-case basis by Parliament with no formal constitutional support. The Chief Justice of the Supreme Court with the power of approval by the President are

Honorable & You: The Government

responsible for nominating Justices throughout the Superior Courts of Judicature.

The Supreme Court is composed of the Chief Justice and at least nine other Justices. Nomination to the Supreme Court requires having practiced law for at least 15 years prior to their nomination. The Court of Appeal is composed of the Chief Justice, and no fewer than ten Justices of the Superior Courts each of whom need to practice at least 12 years of law before they are considered for appointment. The High Court Is made up of the Chief Justice with no less than 20 justices of the High Court and must have completed at least 10 years of legal practice. The Regional Tribunals consist of the Chief Justice, 1 Chairman, and judges chosen by the Chief Justice to sit on the tribunals. The qualifications are the same as The High Court.

The Municipal Chief Executives are responsible for presiding over meetings of the Executive Committee of the Assembly and providing supervision of departments in the Assembly. The Presiding Members main role is to preside over meetings of the General Assembly and make rulings on various procedures. Assembly Members are responsible for maintaining close contact with the electoral area to determine needs and present the views of the electorates to the District Assembly.

 <<<<<Learn more about Ghana's Government

Understanding the technicalities and hierarchal government structure is useful in general so you know the proper protocol and hierarchal order should you ever feel the need to engage the government around accountability for constituent services in your neighborhood. How the rule of law transmits from the top down and is implemented to provide constituent services is murky. Once you become a tax paying citizen and want to hold your government accountable, no matter

Honorable & You: The Government

how murky the process or difficult, you should follow the correct protocol and order.

Like most governments, Ghana can improve greatly on how it actually delivers services to its citizenry and hold the individuals responsible for delivering said services accountable.

While you will find much of Ghana's government is modeled after British and American democracy, although not directly associated, Ghana's traditional leaders and traditional councils have a large influence on political outcomes. They control much of what happens in their traditional areas and have a heavy influence over the people which means votes. They also control and/or manage a lot of land in Ghana. Additionally, you'll find a mixture of traditional symbolism and culture in the government ceremonies.

Symbolism is very important in traditional Ghanaian culture. The symbolism is most notable with the Mace which is a staff similar to that carried by a chief's linguist, carried by the Speaker of Parliament and the President's sword present when he is addressing parliament and making an oath. The sword is a version of the traditional Akofena which stands for statehood and authority and is a kin to the same sword traditional leaders use for their oath of allegiance to serving the people. The Adinkra symbols embossed between the stools on the Mace denote the Omnipotence of God, critical examination, strength, immortality, and justice. These are the symbols on the Mace.

- **THE FLYING EAGLE** - symbolizing the State of Ghana.
- **"KONTONKUROWI"** - symbol of the common sharing of responsibility.
- **"NYAMEDUA"** - a stool symbol of the presence of God in society.
- **"HWEMDUA"** - symbol of critical examination.
- **"GYE-NYAME"** - (except God), a symbol of the omnipotence of God.
- **"KUDU-PONO"** - a symbol of lasting personality.

Honorable & You: The Government

- **"MBAADWA"** - a symbol of the presence and effect of feminine power in society.
- **"DWANIMMEN"** - a symbol of manly strength.
- **"HYE-WO-NHYE"** - (burnt but unburnt), symbol of imperishability.
- **"BI-NKA-BI"** - (no one bites another), symbol of justice.
- **"KUNTUN-KANTAN"** - (bent only to straighten), symbol of the pride of State.

I met Danny Damah through my favorite Ghana WhatsApp groups called 2021 Beyond – (shouts out to Lorraine and Terry). I noticed this brother had a wealth of knowledge by the case at which he spit facts and knowledge about Ghana in general but more impressively where Ghana sits in the world market and the opportunities that exist to collaborate Ghana's government to help build Ghana. So I reached out and asked him to contribute to this guide.

Introducing Danny Damah >>>>>>>>>>

Hi there, I'm sure you have done your research on Ghana and probably read the prior chapters before getting to this one. But I'd like to give you a brief contemporary history of investors in Ghana.

Why should you move to and invest in Ghana?

Ghana is a premier location to do business on the African continent. Present conditions include political stability, a growing economy, increasing consumer demand, accessibility to the wider West African market of close to 400 million and viable local partners. I will take this opportunity to invite potential investors from all over the world, including Ghanaians in the Diaspora, to come and invest in Ghana. Investors in Ghana have recorded average profits in excess of 35% of their total investments. This is a huge return that I urge potential investors to take advantage of in Ghana.

Honorable & You: The Government

It's important to note if you are an African American or diaspora investor (all foreign investors), you are guaranteed unconditional transferability of dividends and net profits after tax to your home countries; transferability of payments for loan servicing in the case of foreign loans and royalties; and other fees in respect of technology transfer transactions. Ghana also guarantees the remittances of proceeds in the event of sale and liquidation of investment assets in the currency in which the investment was originally made to their home countries so far as they meet their tax obligations. An American citizen living and investing in Ghana isn't taxed on the first $75,000 income earned in Ghana. Moreover, Ghana uses the instrumentality of double taxation agreements to protect the affected investors from double taxation by both their home governments and the host country. Please visit the Ghana Investment Promotion Centre.

Ghana has been a global hub since the 14th century. Fast forward to today, Ghana is still a central hub in Africa with a focus on its natural resources. However, an emerging industrial tech scene is growing. Since becoming the first sub-Saharan country to gain independence in 1957, Ghana has been a trailblazer in many fields.

Ghana is the first country in Sub-Saharan Africa to have a satellite launched into orbit. Google's First Artificial Intelligence Centre in Africa was launched in Ghana. A combination of government policy and seeking for greater market share has seen the total subscriptions of 2G/3G/4G mobile data in the country reach over 31 million with a mobile phone penetration rate of 90% (internet 35%). Considered by some to be the gateway to West Africa, many underlying aspects make Ghana an ideal place to do business. Its geographic position as the country closest to the center of the world (GMT & Equator) allows for ease of communication and short flight distances. Compared to its peers of Nigeria, Côte d'Ivoire and Kenya, Ghana performs well on several key metrics such as GDP per capita, percentage of population on the internet and access to electricity.

Ghana's GDP per capita at $4,700 is above Kenya at $3,500 and Côte d'Ivoire at $3,900. Ghana also has a higher percentage of the population with access to the internet (34.7% compared to Nigeria 25.7%, Côte d'Ivoire 26.5% and Kenya 26%). With a very critical infrastructure provision in terms of access to electricity it exceeds the rest with 79% of the population having access to electricity compared to 54.5% in Nigeria, 65.6% Côte d'Ivoire and 63.8% Kenya *(CIA FACTBOOK)*.

Ghana's infrastructure (roads, power, internet), political stability, location and ranking on ease of doing business according to the World Bank all contribute to the attractiveness of Ghana as a business destination. For a country 7 times smaller than Nigeria, Ghana attracted almost double the foreign direct investment (3.5 billion USD to 1.9 billion USD) in 2018. That serves as an indicator of the positive business and investment environment in Ghana.

The Ghanaian government is playing a role in making Ghana a conducive environment for businesses and entrepreneurship to flourish with the focus moving from traditional cottage businesses to industrial including tech entrepreneurship. For this chapter, I'll concentrate on the light agro-processing processing and manufacturing industry.

Ease of Doing Business

Over the years the government has taken strides to establish:

- a digital addressing system, which enables locations to be found readily and has in turn supported the growth of delivery, ride hailing, ecommerce services;

- interoperability of mobile money services, which allows people to pay and receive money from various phone networks thus boosting trade and commerce and catering to a previously unbanked population.

- the National Entrepreneurship and Innovation Plan(NEIP) to drive awareness, engagement and support for entrepreneurs across the country.

- tax breaks for start-ups to enable them to grow and utilize their earnings for reinvestment.

- digitization of various services including the passport service and the ports and harbors in Ghana.

- the Accra Digital Centre, which hosts both the Ghana Innovation Hub and the Ghana Tech Lab which falls under the eTransform program of the Ministry of Communications with funding from the World Bank Group and Rockefeller Foundation.

These digitization efforts provide an indication of the commitment that government has to embracing technology and creating an enabling environment for tech innovations to flourish.

The entrepreneurship ecosystem was dominated by grassroots operators and over the last decade the landscape has changed dramatically. From a few hubs and incubators located in the capital city to over 30 tech and business hubs across the country which means that access to support has increased drastically. There has also been an increase in support from corporates and international agencies.

Industrialization

Things haven't always been easy for the country. Ghana has been through a tumultuous past. 10 years ago Ghana embarked on an industrial journey by starting with the Ghana Industrial Policy.

Honorable & You: The Government

Ghana changed its development focus from a grassroots oriented economy where the core focus was on repairing the damage to our infrastructure from the destructive years of the revolutions to an industrialized self-sustaining economy focused on exporting goods and services.

Ghana Industrial Policy>>>>>>>>>>

The former included basic routine government investments like roads, schools, hospitals, railways, port etc. This also included availability of inputs, spare parts and materials so that ordinary subsistence small holder farmers, petty traders and entrepreneurs could obtain their minimum basic needs within a fair and equitable system. All these measures cost money and whilst they improved many aspects of Ghanaians daily lives, few of them were sustainable and actually put extra money into the pocket of the ordinary man and woman.

This led to a continuous exodus of Ghanaians like me to seek greener pastures internationally. The industrial decline of the 70's and 80's also gave rise to importation of food products, essential goods, and medicines. With no source of taxable trade revenue, the government put almost 45% duties and other taxes on all imports. This reliance on government revenue from imports further impacted the entire national productivity with an over reliance on borrowing from Western countries to balance its budget and to pay for debts on imported goods.

Ghana, once a vibrant economy in the early 60's on par with Taiwan, South Korea and even China, had it all. Ghana was assembling vehicles, busses, farm equipment, televisions, radios and other electronics, textiles and clothing, oil refineries, aluminum smelters & fabrication, sulphur chemical plants, glass blowing, rubber tires manufacturing, medicines and other industrial chemicals, a ship and boatyard, film and television production studios with cinemas across the country and music performance stages, tobacco plants, numerous beer brewery, soda and alcoholic beverage plants, ship repair dry docks, engineering firms, construction materials, leather industries, sugar, palm oil, cocoa and various agro products.

This new focus on two parallel approaches embedded in the government's policy are an export-led industrialization strategy and domestic market-led industrialization strategy based on import competition (import substitution) has leaped frogged Ghana into a land of opportunity and endless potential.

Dealing with Government

For those looking to move into Ghana as industrial investors, the government has a clear vision to partner diaspora investors looking to settle in Ghana. The vision serves the core purpose of technology transfer to build the industrial capacity of the average Ghanaian, whilst creating jobs for its youthful population. You will find out that for an investor, government –at the highest level- is very approachable, as it wants to turn Ghana into a manufacturing hub for West Africa and the Ghana Industrial Policy of 2010 as I referenced in the first paragraph has served as a 'north star' for this. There are many government agencies set up to hand-hold a potential investor through all the business establishment steps.

The Ghana Investment Promotion Centre (GIPC), which sits under the Office of the President, has played an important role since the GIPC Act was passed in 2013. Much of the credit for securing foreign investment in Ghana's manufacturing sector lies with the GIPC Act which enabled the government to provide a set of incentives and subsidies for companies looking to manufacture for export, as well as the policy allowing duty-free import of technology and machinery for manufacturing. Politically, industrialization has become a bipartisan issue in Ghana, with both of the major political parties i.e. the center left NDC and the center right NPP recognizing its electoral popularity and its importance for the country's economic transformation, irrespective of their political ideology.

 <<<<<<<Ghana Investment Promotion Centre

Under both of the major political parties over the last decade, transformative investments were made in infrastructure, an industrial policy was developed, and there was a push to use revenue from the relatively new oil sector to finance an ambitious economic diversification program.

The government has removed important trade barriers, by adhering strictly to its industrial strategy as a coordinating tool to eliminate specific obstacles, such as trade barriers, industrial land availability, and tailored infrastructure, and accentuate the country's strengths –peace and stability, abundance natural industrial resources, the rule of law, a highly-educated workforce, relatively inexpensive labor and availability of key resources.

Recently, the government has prioritized ensuring reliable and cheap power, financial stability and land for investors. Competitively cheap and stable industrial energy has been a priority for all successive Governments. Affordable labor and cheap energy are really what's needed to put Ghana in a competitive advantage against China and South Korea as a manufacturing destination. With the increased production of its own Natural Gas, these policy goals are now within reach.

Ghana has also developed special economic zones such as the Tema Export Processing Zone, which has been remarkably successful and has played a central part in the growth of Ghana's industrial sector over the past decade, with the attraction of companies such as Barry Callebaut, Cargill and Cocoa Touton to the country a direct result of the efforts of the Ghana Free Zones

Honorable & You: The Government

Board. Industrial policy is nothing without implementation and collaboration.

The Government has deliberately focused on working with investors to create markets, supporting local industries and to creating a suitable environment for foreign investment and technology transfer. Two examples of this are the Ministry of Tourism, Culture and Creative Arts working closely with African American investors to boost its socio-cultural tourism industry into an over $3 billion industry and the Ministry of Industry and Trade and other government stakeholders' work over the last 4 years to develop a policy to kickstart a local automotive assembly and manufacturing industry in Ghana.

For others seeking to move to Ghana for less capital intensive industrial investments, the rural parts of Ghana are the answer. Poised for the next wave of multibillion dollar growth rural industrialization. The "One District One Factory" (Please visit their website for more up to date info) initiative is a key component of the Industrial Transformation Agenda of the NPP Government. (The concept was first introduced by the Ministry of Trade, Industry and Presidential Special Initiatives during the past New Patriotic Party (NPP) Administration, as part of an integrated program for Accelerated Growth and Industrial Development.

The District Industrialization Programme (DIP) was designed as a comprehensive program for rural industrialization, involving the setting up of at least one medium to large scale factory in each of the administrative districts of Ghana. While previous attempts at rural economic revitalization in Ghana had focused mainly on the provision of physical infrastructural facilities, the DIP focuses on the promotion of commercially viable business development initiatives, to generate sustainable & accelerated economic development in rural communities, and to encourage new community-based public/private partnerships. It's a great

Honorable & You: The Government

opportunity for a newcomer to invest in communities and utilize their local resources in manufacturing products that are in high demand both locally and internationally. This will allow you to reap the rewards of industrialization, and the country increase its agricultural and manufacturing output, reduce reliance on imports and increase food availability. The program is expected to facilitate the creation of between 7,000 to 15,000 jobs per district and between 1.5 million and 3.2 million jobs nationwide by the end of 2024.

Personal Side Note: Although there's no minimum or maximum one can invest in Ghana, my advice is that it's prudent to have or raise (debt, equity, or mezzanine) of at least $100,000 for a small scale enterprise and between, $250,000 to $1,000,000 for a medium scale industry. When I moved back to Ghana I realized that beyond having Capex and Opex for a business in Ghana, it's important to have at least $25,000 for personal expenses to last you for a year as you develop your business. In Ghanaian broken English we call this "Accra Stay By Plan".

I found out that Ghana is a rather stress free slow paced economic environment, which can be expensive in time wasted on mundane bureaucratic processes. It takes a much longer time to achieve simple goals. It's an age old, accepted practice called Ghana Man Time or GMT. Many foreigners have complained and tried to change this pace, they all tend to accept its stress reducing nature and quickly adapt their businesses activities to the cultural attitude.

While there are a few lucky diaspora entrepreneurs who can rely on their own savings or have wealthy friends or family members who can afford to inject capital, most business owners need to go out of their way to raise funds from outside sources. This leads you to the most important question of business planning in Ghana: "what is my immediate business objective and what resources do I need to make it happen?" Money can definitely help you with getting started, however, in the beginning stages, there are other ways to get support or resources free of cost, one of which is to partner with a resident Ghanaian with similar interests as yours (I'll elaborate more on this approach in a later paragraph) and the other is to approach the government's diaspora affairs office for guidance.

The more you are able to grow your business in this way and convince others to support you, the more appealing it will be to local or international investors or funders in the future. If you are not able to obtain funding from outside sources, you may also consider alternatives on how to grow your business in a lean way. This is known to you in the West as boot-strapping, in Ghana we simply term it "Kpa Kpa kpa hustling". The lean kpa kpa kpa model is often used by most Ghanaians in starting a business, as there are a number of things every entrepreneur needs to do before he or she thinks about fundraising.

Most diaspora entrepreneurs currently in Ghana have been able to bootstrap their start-ups for a significant period of time and achieve adequate growth before needing to turn to an investor for additional capital. However, this often depends on the sector and business model others may need to tap into the friends and family round in order to get their idea off the ground.

One should approach the 1 District 1 Factory initiative from the perspective of competing favorably as an investor/manufacturer with any imported goods in Ghana (in extension West Africa). One has to walk into any supermarket or market stall in Ghana, identify the foreign imported products and brands (it could also simply be a product from your home country or even a new concept or product you have developed) and start on a quest to produce that product locally in Ghana.

Once you've done some research and development, generated a great idea (identified a problem that exists for businesses or

Honorable & You: The Government

consumers in Ghana/West Africa), determine a solution, and think about how to turn that solution into a product or service. This often starts with problems that you have a personal insight to), identified a resource region or district in Ghana (conduct a feasibility study assessing the market size, revenue generation models and potential customer segments), identified its socio-economic impact, its job creation potential and importantly its profitability (create an early version of your product.

While having a great idea is important, it does not always translate into a successful business locally. An important step is to get feedback early about your product. This might be about how and when they use it and how much they are willing to pay for it. This is the first step to determining your product/market fit and how well your product is suited to the Ghana).

Note: It is always advisable to seek a knowledgeable Ghanaian entrepreneur to partner or consultant on your product. Partnering a Ghanaian offers really important benefits including a reduction in minimum investment capital, maintaining favorable communication with goods distributors, gaining access to legally binding local content supply and service contracts, access into other Ecowas (West African) markets, and the ability to access many government subsidies and exemptions reserved for Ghanaians.

It's time to engage the government of Ghana through its 1D1F business incubation programme. Under the 1D1F you will be able to accelerate your industrialization business with the might of government behind you, in any district you wish to settle in. Under the 1D1F you will be given further insight and access to an existing business, consumer or parastatal customer database of ready off-takers for your industrial business.

At this point it is important for me to clarify that the Government of Ghana has put emphasis on certain core industries that have been integral to social development and a drain on the country and region's trade deficit. Most of these industries have local sourced raw material or immediate local human and infrastructural capacity. The key industries include poultry & livestock, fisheries, sheanut, cashew, soya, cocoa, fruits and vegetables, fruit, juices and alcoholic beverages, sugar, milk, rice, wheat substitutes, cooking oils (palm oil, automobile & other transport assembly, soybean oil, coconut oil,) agro processing, constructions materials, Pharmaceuticals, poultry, garments and textiles, iron ore, cement, feldspar, gold, silver, aluminum, and the creative arts.

The government is also interested in the establishment of anchor industries including the petrochemical industry, cheap renewable energy and the manufacturing of machinery equipment and components. 1D1F is not limited to these industries and their value chains, but the government is keen on ending the income deficit associated with these industries

For a Diasporan moving to Ghana there is good news to raise capital locally for industrial purposes with the assistance of the 1D1F secretariat. There are a number of financial institutions set up to assist the 1D1F initiative key amongst which is the Ghana Exim Bank.

<<<<<<Visit 1District 1 Factory Site

Ghana EXIM Bank is the driving force behind Ghana's agenda of transforming the country into an export-hub, through industrialization and support for the private sector using several initiatives like the 1D1F. In choosing enterprises it would support; Ghana EXIM Bank considers three key benchmarks which are derived from development instead of commercial objectives.

These are employment creation, value addition through production efficiency and foreign exchange revenue potential. Exim Bank's Lending Rate lending rate is the lowest in the industry at 8% per

Honorable & You: The Government

annum to support export and strategic importation. Each sector the Bank finances is selected based on the potential competitiveness in the West African Sub-region and indeed Africa as a whole.

1D1F has supported the setup of 230 factories in different stages of completion, 119 of which were funded either wholly or in part by the Exim Bank. As a Diasporan the type of funding you can get from the Exim bank includes Agricultural Finance, Asset Finance, Working Capital Finance, Performance Guarantee, Retention Bond, Project Finance, Advance Payment Guarantee etc. The bank would give credit support to, crop and fish farming, cost harvest management, processing, branding and packaging research and development, aggregation and distribution (distribution networks, transport and logistics) and export facilitation of local farm/processing equipment R&D, manufacturing, assembly and leasing industry.

It's clear to see that Ghana's future is in innovative industrialization. The initiatives taken by Government of Ghana to support diaspora investors is a major step in assuring innovative entrepreneurs of a supportive funding partner when they come into the country. Regardless of where innovative entrepreneurs come from or live in Ghana, the assistance from the Ghana government is accessible and provides the new Ghanaian transplant with a very bright future.

Honorable & You: The Government

Check out Ntansa if you need Business Process Automation

MANAGING BANDS: MONEY & FINANCE

One of my favorite quotes is, "Money ain't everything but it's up there with breathing." Money and financial transactions are important in life. These two feel more important in Ghana because Ghana – like many countries in Africa - is still a cash-based society. Credit and loans are not readily available. Where available, they're very expensive. Money can cost 20% annually on average. Despite the rise and popularity of mobile money, credit cards, and crypto currency, cash is still king in Ghana. Having access to cash when you need it – in dollars, cedis, euros or pounds can often make things happen more quickly.

From the moment you get off the plane and begin moving through the country, it seems that someone is asking for money at every turn. The assumption is that because you're a foreigner, you have money in excess. It's important to note that not all Ghanaians are money hungry and want you to give them a handout. However, it is also important to note that the majority of Ghana is poor. As a repatriate, refraining from making general and absolute statements such as "Ghanaians do this or that", will go a long way in helping you to adjust to life in a country where poverty is rampant, and for many, unceasing. Know that many are managing the best they can.

Constant requests for money can get frustrating. Whether from the police at the random road stops who have their way of asking "something for your boys" or the security guard who opens the door at the bank; or the customer service rep at the phone store; or the cashier at the grocery store. It often feels that someone always has their hand out. Interestingly enough, I've traveled somewhat extensively throughout West Africa and every country with high poverty doesn't have the same culture around money. I've found that Ghana is much more aggressive around money. My experience has been that the unabashed demands for money

Managing Bands: Money & Finance

without exchange of goods or service is one unique to Ghana. This is changing for the better as more of us from Diaspora repatriate and have open conversations about what rebuilding Ghana together means.

African Americans and the Black diaspora do need to come to terms with the fact that our longing to return to the continent of Africa may be for different reasons than many indigenous Africans have for advocating for our return. We are the grassroots African stimulus package. We are not being welcomed with open arms by the government and people just because they miss us and believe at their core that Africa is our birthright as we do. And its ok. We can figure out how to make it work for the good of the Global Black order.

Please do not be confused about this. Sit with this. Let it marinate. And get clear quickly or it will cause an unnecessarily frustrating internal conflict about something that is simply reality. And after you sit with it, know that it's ok. You get to choose how much of this part of the reality of returning you will allow to become a part of your daily life. It will be your responsibility to balance your journey with what you think, what you want and what is. There are going to be people you meet who are genuine and others who are looking for a payday. Keep your antennae sharp and pay attention. In general, people who put the transaction before the relationship are just looking for a payday.

The currency in Ghana is based on the Ghanaian cedi (currency symbol GH¢) and the pesewa (currency symbol Gp). Pesewas are the basic units of Ghanaian currency and cedis are the second tier. Pesewas are comparable to the United States penny and the cedi is comparable to a United States dollar. However, the cedi is of a lower monetary value than currency in the United States. The current exchange rate is 1 Ghanaian cedi to 17 cents or one US dollar to 5.75 Ghanaian cedi. The cedi's value fluctuates daily . A

Managing Bands: Money & Finance

part of daily life as a repatriate is checking the value of Ghanaian currency. The cedi is available in notes of 1ghc, 2ghc, 5ghc, 10ghc, 20ghc, 50ghc, 100ghc and 200ghc.

The per capita GDP for Ghana between 2019 – 2020 was about $1900. Comparatively, it was $65,000 in the US, $45,000 Canada and $42,000 UK. As of 2020, the daily minimum wage in Ghana stood at 11.82 Ghanaian cedis (GHS) (approximately 2.03 U.S. dollars), representing an increase of 1.17 GHS (around 0.2 U.S. dollars) from 2019. 11.82 ghc daily minimum wage means the average person in Ghana makes about $2 per day. So obviously the need and want for money is real.

Knowing and understanding the culture around money and how it's leveraged in Ghana can make all the difference in the world for you, your family, and/or your business/investment partners.

Banking

Banking in Ghana is interesting. The banks are often very crowded, and transactions that we would consider to be routine or basic take a much longer time to process. There also isn't much privacy for patrons conducting bank business however, there is a space for a higher level of person-to-person customer service you'll never get in America. I bank with both Fidelity and UBA. For those conducting business in Ghana, It's common to have accounts with several banks.

Check out Fidelity Bank in Ghana>>>>>>>

As a foreign national interested in opening a bank account in Ghana, you must first a have residency permit and/or work permit. You can open a joint account with a local Ghanaian without being a legal resident. I don't suggest this unless you know the person really well. My first account was a joint account with a person with whom I am extremely comfortable. It's

Managing Bands: Money & Finance

important to note, however, that our relationship is one that is built on high levels of accountability and integrity on a business and spiritual level.

The process of acquiring a bank account requires you to be physically present and is as simple as completing a number of forms for the bank, including an IRS W-9 form. You will need a copy of your passport, residency permit and two passport sized photos. Most banks will offer both a cedi account and a dollar account so you can bank in the currency you choose.

Under each type of account, you can get a current account - the American equivalent of a checking account. Also available are savings accounts and at most banks – some sort of investment account. Most banks also offer government bond investment accounts and have a high return of 15 – 20% but require you to keep your funds invested for set periods of time and may have penalties for withdrawal. The investment accounts will differ per bank. Most banks in Ghana offer mobile banking apps, online banking, and will provide a checkbook and/or Visa or Master Card ATM/debit cards.

Most banks will also assign you a customer relationship manager. This is normally the banker at your branch who helped you complete your paperwork and processed your account. Your relationship manager will be responsible for clearing your bank wires, can help you when you're in a rush and the bank lines are long, do banking on your behalf, assist with business banking, and present your case for a loan with the bank should you need that. I appreciate the personalized service that is part of the standard banking experience in Ghana. It will be extremely convenient for you to open an account somewhere near your home so you can do your primary banking at your home branch.

You can wire or physically deposit dollars or cedis into your prospective accounts. Note that when you wire cedis your bank will convert the dollars at the standard bank rate for that day to cedis. When you wire dollars to your dollar account in Ghana, you will pay 3% of the total wire which is deducted over time with each transaction. You currently do not have to pay the 3% on dollars you physically deposit into the bank.

To be clear, if you walk in and deposit dollars and wire dollars, you will have two different dollar deposits from which you can withdraw and spend – one will cost you 3% and the other will cost you nothing. The United States government allows you to legally travel from the US to Ghana with up to $10,000 of undeclared funds. If you plan to stack dollars in your account in Ghana, you'll have to make several trips to do so or pay the 3%.

You may use your ATM card In Ghana. Money is always dispersed in Ghana cedis and you may be charged significant fees from the ATM and your own bank. I absolutely do not suggest using ATMs at all if it can be avoided.

Mobile Money (Momo)

Mobile money is similar to Paypal, CashApp and Zelle; cash is deposited into your digital wallet from a mobile money vendor or a deposit from your account into your mobile money wallet. You do not have to have a bank account for mobile money. There are several different mobile money brands in Ghana: MTN, Vodafone, and Airtel/Tigo are the main vendors. Each a full-service telecommunications company with products and services including phones, tablets, wifi modems, internet, data and business enterprise packages will also have their own mobile money network. Momo – the largest mobile money network is MTN's mobile money, Vodacash is the second-largest mobile money network, and is operated by Vodafone.

Managing Bands: Money & Finance

You must have a valid residency permit to register your phone number for a mobile money account, and you must keep your SIM card and mobile money account active. Your mobile money account is connected to your SIM card, phone number, and can be connected to your bank account. You can use your mobile money account through phone prompts or the app if a company has an app. For example, for MTN Momo you dial *170# and press send (call) to access your menu of features.

Download MTN Mobile Money>>>>>>>

Mobile money apps allow you complete a wide array of everyday tasks from the palm of your hand. With mobile money, you may add data to your phone line, send money to a friend, pay for your home internet (broadband), purchase groceries, gas, and clothing and much more. Some landlords and development companies even accept it for rent, lease and purchase. Many other business services offer mobile money as an easy way to pay.

Using mobile money isn't free. Unless you are depositing or withdrawing money at a bank, each mobile money transaction incurs a fee based on the transaction amount. If you're moving to Ghana, having your own mobile money account that is registered to you and in your full control over is essential and prevents you from always having to carry cash.

You can also use money sending apps like Sendwave once your Momo account is set up to help send yourself money when in need. Sendwave sends the cedi equivalent direct to a mobile money account from your US bank account or debit card. You're able to send yourself mobile money direct from your own US bank account to your own mobile money account. You should set up your Sendwave account before departing the US.

<<<<<<Download Sendwave

Money Exchange

You can change money at a bank, a Forex location, or on the black market. Most people who have moved to Ghana have a personal money exchange agent or two and/or a place where they exchange regularly. All banks can complete foreign exchange but the rate is normally lower in the bank than through the Forex or black market. Black market exchange will almost always return the best rate and can normally accommodate the exchange any amount of money. If you're exchanging money on the black market, be careful to use a recommended person and don't travel to unfamiliar areas. Black market exchange also means there is no way to track the origin of counterfeit bills, should they show up in your hands.

When traveling to Ghana, note that new $100 and $50 bills with a date after 2009 will get the highest exchange rates. Dollar bills in denominations of 20 are accepted sometimes but will always get you a much lower exchange rate. Ten dollar, $5 and $1 bills are rarely accepted and if they are, the rate will be even lower than $20s.

Be aware that the exchange rate will vary around the country. You'll almost always get the best exchange rate in Accra. Sometimes the rate will differ by a whole cedi but most times the difference is smaller. Exchanging $100 at 5.7 vs 5.75 will only net a difference of 5 cedis, so it may not make sense to go out of your way for such a small amount. However $5,000 at 5.7 vs 5.75 is a difference of 250 ghc.

Finally, it's also important to think and act in Ghana cedis. This means you don't think in dollars and convert to cedis. You move the opposite way. It may "only" be $50 but it's also 275 cedis. Thinking and operating in Cedis means you're making decisions based on the local market and cost of living in Ghana, not the United States. This takes some time to become second nature. Familiarity with the market and understanding functional cost of living will come as you live and operate in cedis. There are levels to understanding money operationally and functionally in Ghana that only comes with time.

LIVING LEGAL: CITIZENSHIP, RESIDENCY & PERMITS

One of the biggest misunderstandings that came with the Year of Return was that Ghana would grant dual citizenship to people visiting Ghana during 2019 simply because they are persons of African descent. I have read posts on Facebook that Ghana was giving citizenship to people who bought land. I've also seen articles that state Ghana is giving citizenship to people of African descent who trace their ancestry to Ghana. Unfortunately, It's all fake news.

The Ghanaian government has had two citizenship conferment ceremonies in the past four years. Both were at the will of the sitting President, who by executive order, decided to confer citizenship on Africans of the diaspora living in Ghana. The first was former President of Ghana John Mahama who gave citizenship to 34 Africans of the diaspora residing in Ghana. The second was the current President, His Excellency Nana Addo Dankwa Akufo Addo. In December 2019, he granted citizenship to 126 Diasporan Africans currently residing in Ghana as part of the Year of Return. This granting of citizenship was the result of the tireless efforts of many people who lobbied the government and worked behind the scenes for years.

Contrary to many of the rumors floating about, there is no current law, process, or method that streamlines or automatically qualifies Black people to become citizens of Ghana strictly because we are descendants of Africa. Individuals wishing to become citizens currently must follow the rules and regulations from the Ghanaian government for naturalization. However, there are ongoing efforts to lobby the Ghanaian government for a streamlined citizenship process which includes people of African descent. The Homeland Return Act, currently under development, is said to include a process that will streamline citizenship for Africans of the diaspora

Legal Living: Citizenship, Residency & Permits

currently living in Ghana, or those interested in moving and obtaining citizenship.

I strongly discourage anyone interested in gaining dual citizenship in Ghana from paying a fee or working with any one particular group promising citizenship outside of the current naturalization process. However, I do encourage you to explore all the options and at least attend meetings and sessions on citizenship. The most anyone can do for you is add your name to a prospective list of potential candidates that may be considered for citizenship if the sitting president decides to confer citizenship again. My suggestion is to visit the Office of Diaspora Affairs at the Office of the President and follow their directions.

Review the naturalization process>>>>>

In the meantime, to become a legal resident, you must obtain a residency permit - which is different from the visa required to enter Ghana for US citizens. There are different categories of visas - including diplomatic, business, tourist, student and family (spouse or child of Ghanaian national). If you are moving for work or enrolling in school, your job or school authority will normally guide you through this process. If not, the best and easiest method that requires the least amount of documentation is the tourist visa. Once in Ghana, after visiting and exploring, you can apply for the necessary residency and/or business documentation should you decide to move, stay and/or engage in business.

There are three licensed authorities in the US that can grant tourist visas for entry to Ghana: the Ghana Embassy in Washington, DC, the Ghana Consulate in New York, and the honorary Consulate of Ghana in Houston, Texas. Each has its own requirements for a tourist visa, but all visas issued provide the same rights. You can apply for a single or multiple-entry visa. A single-entry visa allows you to enter the country one time and stay for up to 60 consecutive

Legal Living: Citizenship, Residency & Permits

days. This means you cannot travel to another country and re-enter Ghana. A multiple-entry visa allows you to come and go as you please, entering the country as many times as you want, for a maximum of 60 consecutive days through the expiration date of your visa.

You do not get to choose the duration of your multiple-entry visa. That decision rests solely with the consular officer of the location processing your visa, but the maximum is 5 years. I encourage all who are serious about being on the ground in Ghana to pay the $40 difference between the single and multiple-entry visa. If you overstay your visa beyond 60 days, there is currently a small fee of 80ghc per 30 days that must be paid before your return to your home country.

<<<<<<Visit the Ghana Embassy in DC Site

To obtain a residency permit, you must apply while you're on the ground in Ghana. There are several different types of residency and work permits depending on your situation. If you're traveling and moving for a job, it's best to allow your employer to guide and manage that process or you.

The residency permit is an actual sticker in your passport, so you will need to submit your passport, two passport photos, a police report from your country of origin, a medical report from a recognized hospital in Ghana, and the various forms and application required. I highly encourage anyone coming on their own looking to get residency to work with a vetted company or source on the ground to assist you with the process.

An internet search for Ghana residency permit will lead you to valuable information but it can still be a bit confusing. You can't download the forms from the site or pay for them online. Your application must be approved through the Ghana Immigration Service and Ministry of the Interior but finding out which building,

Legal Living: Citizenship, Residency & Permits

office, and when they're open can also be a bit confusing unless you physically go there. The cost is about $1000 for the one year residency permit.

It's important to renew your residency permit annually after your first year to maintain and keep your record of legal residency. After you've maintained legal residency for 5 years, you can then apply for permanent residency, which is required for naturalization.

Learn more about Residency Permits>>>>>>

For those interested in driving in Ghana, you'll need to get a driver's license. If you have a current, valid drivers from your home state, you should be able to go to the Driver and Vehicle Licensing Authority (DVLA), convert your license to a Ghanaian license. If you don't have a license or it is expired, you'll have to complete the process from the beginning. Fortunately, getting a driver's license is fairly simple and the DVLA has a number of processes you can complete online.

<<<<<<<<Connect with the DVLA online to convert your driver's license

DIRTY GAMES: LAND, REAL ESTATE & RENTING

Real estate is property made up of land and the buildings on it, as well as the natural resources of the land including uncultivated flora and fauna, farmed crops and livestock, water, and any additional mineral deposits. There are essentially four types of real estate.

Residential real estate includes both the new construction and resale of single family homes, condominiums, co-ops, townhouses, duplexes, triple-deckers, quadplexes, high-value homes, and vacation homes. Commercial real estate includes shopping centers and strip malls, medical and educational buildings, hotels, offices, and apartment buildings although they are used for residences because they are owned to produce income.

Industrial real estate includes manufacturing buildings, properties and warehouses that can be used for research, production storage, and distribution of goods. Land includes vacant land, working farms and ranches. Combined with Ghana's continued infrastructural development, a safer business environment and the countries growing international appeal, the real estate sector will be one of the leading sectors to propel the country forward and can be an investor's dream.

Before investing, it is important to understand the market in Ghana. Real estate in Ghana may be the most researched topic for repatriates because one of the first things you need to do is secure a place to live. And for those looking to build wealth through investment, real estate is a popular avenue. But you'll really need to take your time. Whether you're buying land and building a house for your family and/or investment; buying a condo or renting short or long term, you need to take your time and research. Unfortunately, there is a ton of misinformation and a lot of people who prey on innocent and under-informed souls looking to reconnect with the Motherland.

The real estate market in Ghana is growing rapidly and doesn't look or feel like it will slow down anytime soon. With a ballooning deficit of 2 million housing units, the demand for real estate in Ghana can only continue to grow. In that demand lies an incredible investment opportunity for people who can stomach the process and market inconsistencies to make great returns and help stand in the gap for both Ghanaians and foreigners looking to call Ghana home.

Real Estate in Ghana>>>>>>>>

While the majority of real estate development and growth as we know it is focused on Accra, according to the Ghana Investment Promotions Council (GIPC), Kumasi and Takoradi- the next two most populous cities in Ghana - are emerging to offer growing real estate development opportunities.

In many ways, the real estate market in Ghana is sustained by real estate agents, as every important faction of the sector relies on them. While there isn't any officially recognized body for real estate agents in Ghana, and Ghanaian law loosely regulates the real estate industry, the Ghana Real Estate Professionals Association (GREPA) and the Ghana Association of Real Estate Brokers (GAREB) are the two leading the charge. Developers are the best bet for those looking to live in well-planned, gated communities with good roads, 24/7 security, basic amenities, and uniform designs. These developments also have the best chance of being considered for mortgages because they work directly with banks and home financiers. Development is capital-intensive so there aren't that many reputable companies. The downside is that of those that exist, many are not Black-owned and it's hard to find the quality they offer elsewhere.

Dirty Games: Land, Real Estate & Renting

Online marketplaces exist but the biggest problem with online platforms is a lack of transparency and authenticity as online scams are difficult to regulate. Beware of completing and executing any agreements through online portals.

<<<<<<<<<<Check out GREPA

Prior to the Year of Return and the COVID-19 pandemic, you couldn't find a lot of useful and direct information on the internet. However, now that many agents, YouTube bloggers, and other influencers were forced to operate and figure out how to share information virtually, you'll find a lot of useful content around real estate in Ghana online. However, let's remain clear that there is no adequate replacement for boots on the ground. You should know that land disputes are the biggest, longest, and nastiest court cases in Ghana - hands down. If there is any area where you do not want to compromise finding and working with a trusted source on the ground, it's real estate. We'll start with renting and work our way through the ecosystem.

Renting

Renting in Ghana can make all the difference in the world with regard to your repatriation experience. For many this is the first real serious challenge and determines if you decide to keep pushing or pack up and go home. Most residential landlords will require rent in advance up to 24 months and commercial properties can require 3 – 5 years in advance. So if you're paying $750 per month for example, you need to have $18,000 in cash ready to pay for rent. Although this is illegal, it's barely enforced and there's no real recourse. And once you pay your money, there will be no refunds even if you find something different in your rental than what you've agreed, or even if you've included a refund policy in your agreement. Refunds are very rare in Ghana with any transaction, especially anything dealing with real estate. The money

Dirty Games: Land, Real Estate & Renting

exchanging hands is often just a pass-through, and more than likely already spent.

Having a landlord or management company that understands the standard of living you're seeking or to which you're accustomed; is consistently responsive, and proactive; and fully understands and owns their duty as your landlord - is the most important thing you should look for in rental property. Many times the person you meet who is showing you the property, answering your questions, and corresponding with you is not the landlord - regardless of what they say. They are the caretaker of the property or someone the owner or landlord has put in place. Property management companies are going to be the best rental relationships most of the time, but will also have additional fees and be more expensive.

Be diligent in asking every question and spelling everything out in your agreement even if things seem obvious to you. There are no obvious assumptions that matter - only what you put down on paper. For example, if you're renting a furnished house or apartment, you need to define "furnished" and ask for a list of items to be included by room.

<<<<<<<Tenancy Agreements in Ghana

Make sure you understand the water source. Is it underground city water? Is there a well? If so, is there an electronic water pump? Is there a generator for the water pump? Do the owners pay to have water brought in and if so, how often? How many polytanks are used for how many apartments? Are there times of the day or days of the week when water will be off? Ask about average monthly electricity costs. Is there an additional charge for air conditioning?

There are no underground natural gas lines in Ghana. You will need to find out the closest place to fill the gas canisters you'll use to cook if your stove does not run on electricity. Ask if they plan on doing any construction any time soon.

In this situation you can't afford to worry about sounding and feeling like a privileged American. If anything, this is where you own that privilege and allow it flourish. This will be your physical home and headquarters and you want to make sure you have the level of comfort you desire. During your process and conversations about renting, almost everything you request and ask for will be a yes and no problem but remain diligent.

The landlord's main objective most times is to get you to pay, so you want to make sure before you pay, they understand your expectations. You will need to outline how you will communicate, what the process will be for repairs, and what the process will be when/if the landlord doesn't take care of their responsibility. Make sure you put everything in writing no matter how ridiculous it may seem. You will have an experience with something that goes awry, wrong, or doesn't make sense. You can't do anything about that but you can prepare as best as possible by thinking forward and making sure you have already worked out how you will address challenges as they arise.

Buying Land In Ghana

Everybody wants to own their own piece of the dirt on the continent, and it's important. Ownership is key because you can better control your destiny. And because we've been locked and tricked out of so much in America, we want to make sure we can take advantage of that opportunity in Ghana and control our destiny. Buying land in Ghana is not simple and can be very confusing and is unfortunately marred with corruption, malfeasance and often times straight up dishonesty and theft. Many people in Ghana sell the same plots of land to different people intentionally, so you really have to be careful. Sometimes it's not intentional just disorganized efforts and the results of too many chefs in the kitchen.

There are three main types of land in Ghana – Family Land, Stooled Land and Personal Land. There are different rules associated with each type of land and the rules for each type of land may also vary depending on the region or area.

Family Land is land that was passed down or willed to individuals or groups of individuals in a family. For example: a father may pass down land to his three sons. In this case, all three sons own the land and it can only be sold if all three sons agree. Instances where land may have been in the family for hundreds of years, you must have the official elders and/or family representative(s) signature for it be sold properly. And it's often difficult to figure out who is that person or people. Family land could also be managed by a chief or traditional council.

Personal Land is land that is held by a single owner and has no encumbrances, associated family members, government liens, partners, and/or co-owners. Personal land can be owned by a person or a business who has the sole authority over said land and can make the decision to sell alone.

Stooled Land is land owned by the community or a specific group of families who may have first settled on the land hundreds of years ago. Or land that was owned by a chief and has been passed down generationally to the heirs of the stool. Stooled Land is entrusted to the Chief who sits on the governing stool of the traditional council that governs the specific area or group of people. In these instances we're talking about a lot of land - hundred and thousands of acres. The chief with their traditional council is entrusted as caretakers of the land and often allow the community to use it for farming. Chiefs do sell or "lease" stooled land for the "benefit" of the community.

Dirty Games: Land, Real Estate & Renting

Depending on where you buy land in Ghana and what type of land you are buying, the process will include some or all of the steps/items listed below. Once you've completed most of these steps, your final and most difficult step will be registering the land in your name which can take years. The steps listed below are ordered sequentially for an ideal process but things don't always happen this way

1. Land Survey
2. Lands Commission Certification of ownership (free from encumbrance)
3. Indenture with signatures and fingerprints
4. Bill of Sale and/or deed (from previous owner)
5. Court Affidavit (verification of authenticity)
6. Receipt for payment (sometimes this is the indenture)
7. Registering Land

The ideal situation is working with an agent and/or a lawyer familiar with Ghanaian land laws but more importantly someone who has great existing relationships with the other players involved and active partnerships with reputable builders. Pursuing this process alone is not recommended even for experienced real estate professionals in other markets. Heavy lifting is required.

Land in Ghana is considered leased land. Even when you own it free and clear it will still be titled a land lease. Technically, Ghanaians can own or "lease" land for a maximum of 99 years and Non-Ghanaian citizens can own or "lease" land for a maximum of 50 years however each "lease" can be automatically renewed at the end of the stated period for a very small and minimal fee but not automatically renewed in perpetuity.

When you purchase land you receive an indenture which is essentially your land title or deed that indicates the agreed upon price, "lease" duration, location, official size most often in percent of acreage or hectares and any other rules associated with the land. There is always room for several signatures of purchaser, seller, witness, Chief, lawyer and/or representative of the land.

The indenture alone means absolutely nothing without a stamped, certified land search from the regional lands commission confirming that the particular parcel of land is indeed registered to the individual selling it, and that there are no government, family, chiefly, or any other owners that would prevent the land from being sold or cause a problem in the future. There should be an official survey of the land with trackable GPS coordinates outlining the official land boundaries. There may also be a deed, bill of sale from previous ownership, and a stamped and signed court affidavit by a circuit court judge certifying the authenticity of the documents depending on the type of land.

Buying Land in Ghana>>>>>>>>>>

Our connection to and having land as our birthright is one of the things we lost in our kidnaping. For those of us repatriating now who are reclaiming their birthright, land is one of the things we are looking for to help create and establish a family legacy. So despite the sometimes tumultuous terrain, we have to stay focused and keep our eyes on the prize.

Building and Buying Homes in Ghana

Ghana is a cash and carry country which means the bulk of most home building and buying requires cash. There is no standard advanced mortgage or loan process in place to help with first time home buyers. Most banks do not offer what we consider a traditional mortgage with a low percentage down payment and 15 – 30 year monthly payment plan based on a credit score. Although there are some mortgage schemes available, the down payments and interest rates are really high and unaffordable. Money is

Dirty Games: Land, Real Estate & Renting

expensive in Ghana with interest rates averaging anywhere from 18 – 30% for most banks.

I haven't had any direct, personal experience with buying a home in Ghana but I can assure you, as I have reiterated throughout, working with a trusted individual on the ground is paramount to a successful purchase -specifically, someone who is a general contractor or who has a wealth of experience with construction in Ghana. You can definitely learn on the go while doing your own research, but most will not have the bandwidth or patience. While there are regulations for home construction, again, they are loosely regulated at best. Regulation in Accra and the more popular neighborhoods is more heavily regulated than you will find in greater Accra and the deeper suburban areas and villages.

Finding and understanding who regulates what and the previous history of a pre-owned home can be nerve wrecking. Newer homes within community developments managed by property management or the property development firms themselves are your best bet to avoid undetectable existing challenges with pre-owned homes but they will also be the most expensive. You get what you pay for rings true a lot in Ghana.

Determining the value of a home can be difficult to ascertain on your own because there isn't a fully comprehensive online portal available like MLS.com for Ghana where you can pull comps based on square footage, rooms, amenities and similar properties purchases based on proximity. While you can find some homes on MLS.com in Accra and other parts of Ghana, there isn't an MLSAccra.com focused on Ghana.

Because most buildings are concrete, your electrical wires and plumbing are sealed in concrete walls so if there is a challenge with electricity or plumbing, solving it is a bit more involved than we are accustomed to. Home buying and building should be pursued with a maintenance plan involved. Other items to be considered are the

Dirty Games: Land, Real Estate & Renting

source of water and electrical power. If you're home uses city water, you should think about a backup source in case there is shortage or the water is temporarily off. Dumsor (power outages) in the main sections of Accra and other parts of Ghana; and the lack of electricity in many rural or suburban areas are also a challenge, so consider generators and/or solar power.

My first building, currently in process, is a 12-bedroom guest house built on 4 plots of land outside of Accra in a small village. The land where I am building within the 4 plots was gifted to me inside of an existing compound. This is no ordinary place or piece of land. This building is in phase one of a 3-phase construction that includes developing the entire compound into a 45-room retreat/heath center for people of African descent to come for healing, rejuvenation and reconciliation. I've already dug a borehole so we have well water and very soon will extend the full electrical current to the compound and install a generator. We are definitely installing our own solar farm to harness the sun's energy and store power. This is both environmentally friendly and economical.

I've documented and followed the building process from the first ground break through our current phase where we are ready for windows, doors, tiling, trimmings and fixings. I work with a general contractor who brought the carpenter and sub-contracts the masons, plumbers and electricians. While we have a great working relationship, it's not without challenges;. ,I've been able to work with him building small-small over the past couple of years to arrive at where we are today. I am not a professional builder by trade or training, but I am familiar with basic home maintenance and how things work so this first project was an intentional learning experience on how to build in Ghana.

Our first building project>>>>>>>>>>

Dirty Games: Land, Real Estate & Renting

I purposely had my contractor break down the building materials and labor costs for each floor by line item and provide written quotes. I took the time to research costs for supplies myself and compare prices, quality, and availability. And where I couldn't, I required receipts. Moreover, I took the time to work with the general contractor to get to know him, his family and his building style. Most times when we hit a wall and didn't agree, it was because he would say we don't do things like that here. When there wasn't a logical, scientific or functional reason other than that's not how we do things, I would overrule him and introduce my concept in style, design, or function, and work with him to make sure it was done to my specifications.

Another useful resource was having conversations, comparing notes, and not being afraid to say I don't know and ask for help with friends who know more about building than me. One such person is my next guest author who was my first landlord for my first official apartment in Ghana. Watching Gabriel finish the apartment and work on the other buildings inspired me. He also gave me advice on a number of design and building concepts.

Introducing Gabriel Ammah >>>>>>>>

They say "love doesn't cost a thing..." but the investment I put into the love I have for real estate has cost me greatly. I will explain later on. As a first generation Ghanaian born in England, I find my position living in Ghana at the age of forty five fraught with ambiguity. I wasn't always fascinated with the idea of returning back to the country of my parents and my forefathers but something inside me longed for my narrative to be told by myself and that of my people.

My background for the better part of twenty five years was working as a songwriter and music producer in the United Kingdom. Although the industry seemed to be promising at times, I always knew there was a greater calling for my life, that involved making a large difference to people that looked like me.

As a proud husband to a beautiful African-American wife, with two teenagers and a three year old daughter, life couldn't be more adventurous. While living in Tampa, Florida, my wife and I started planning towards our final move to Ghana, we set the wheels in motion in 2016 with the commencement of the first project; a three story-apartment building. I had completed a few training courses while living in the UK, covering multiple trades in carpentry, bricklaying, and plumbing as well as achieving a university degree as a mature student.

Although I had worked on a few home refurbishment jobs in my spare time, I had never project managed a development of this magnitude. If there was any good thing I have learnt from having a "western education" is the ability to query, plan, analyze, and execute without second guessing my ability. That said, my wife and I started detailing everything we needed for the building. We searched online for all the latest equipment we could use for construction, taking into consideration that the electricity voltage is different than what we were using in Florida. We purchased the following items from various online stores:

- Step Down voltage regulator (to convert 110v to 220v)
- Router table (to smooth the edges of tables and doors)
- Miter Saw (to cut timber)
- Bench planer (to smooth out the planks of wood)
- Bench Saw
- Drills, staple guns, paint spraying machine, nail gun
- Shower heads, curtains, bed linen, paint.
- Spirit levels and sledgehammers.

This is just a short list of things we prepared to ship to Ghana to start the project. Most of our items were sent to Ghana through a

Dirty Games: Land, Real Estate & Renting

trusted agent in Tampa who provides a door-to-door service from the East Coast to most locations in Ghana.

As far as land was concerned, I inherited a portion of land that belonged to my father of which he inherited from his late father. In order to commence work on the family land, I negotiated with other senior family members, so as to uphold the uniformity of the existing structures on the land as well as conduct refurbishment work on the old structure that was built by my grandfather.

One of the first snags I had with regards to building in Ghana was to acquire a construction workforce I knew I could trust. Unfortunately, those of us coming from the west have a certain level of romanticism with the notion of Africa and African people being loving and embracing, especially because we look alike. That myth was blown away within the first few days into my project.

Certain tools that I brought over to Ghana to make the work easier for the laborers and bricklayers suddenly went missing. I thought I was doing a humanitarian thing by providing modern equipment, but unfortunately the workers saw otherwise. I soon learned to allow the workers to use the tools they were used to but slowly introduce easier work patterns to encourage better productivity.

Another thing I had to learn very quickly was that the Ghanaian currency is never stable against the dollar. If you are working to a set budget, it's very important to add another 20% on top to make room for the fluctuation in currency and the cost of both material increase and petrol (gas). You might not think it adds up but it surely does. Ever since I started my project, I witnessed the cost of materials increase five times. Quite recently, the cost of a bag of cement was 38 Ghana Cedis. The following month, it increased between Ghs 45- Ghs 48 in most places in Accra.

It is always advisable to bring or buy your own vehicle from the United States or from Europe, preferably a truck. I have a Ford F-

Dirty Games: Land, Real Estate & Renting

150 for a number of reasons. When buying materials from the store or marketplace, the local delivery drivers will charge you premium just because they hear an accent and assume you have a lot of money. I spent a lot of money on deliveries and in the end, I decided to ship my truck over. It functions both as my personal vehicle and my delivery truck, saving me money in the process. This doesn't stop the local delivery drivers from suggesting you should use them.

One important point I would like to make is the issue with the cost of labor. Locally called "workmanship," labor is relatively cheap compared to what you would normally pay in the west but you still have to be mindful not to disturb the local market by increasing the wages of the workers. This may sound a little harsh but I learned the hard way very quickly. Try and understand it from this perspective: a bricklayer (block mason) gets paid on average Ghs70 - Ghs80 a day, a laborer, Ghs50. These prices are reflective of what is being charged as of April 2021. If you increase the wage because you have converted it into the US Dollar or UK sterling, that would be the biggest mistake you can ever make. Yes it may seem low but imagine if you work in Ghana and are paid in the local currency, will you be able to pay your workers a higher wage? It is also not fair on the general population who have to struggle to make a decent wage.

Usually, when you are about to start your project, you have to submit your plans to the local municipal assembly for planning permission. You have to submit your architectural drawings as well as the soil test, structure assessment and registered land documents in order for your plans to be approved. A side note here is that there is an unofficial route to start your project, which will involve paying a bribe to the building inspectors so that they will look the other way. Some reading this may ask, "why is he revealing all this information?" I am simply revealing the truth of what is actually happening on the ground and what my personal

Dirty Games: Land, Real Estate & Renting

experience of conducting business in Ghana has brought me to. I would never suggest paying a bribe but the unfortunate thing in most of Africa is that things are never straight forward, especially when you want to go through the correct channels to get things done.

Having to watch over every trades person is another issue you might find when building in Ghana. The level of detail you would want your property to have, the local tradesmen don't see it that way. A point to take into consideration is the majority of the "skilled" workers do not live in nice properties themselves so having to get them to see your vision of clean lines and functional space is a concept that most will not understand. I have taken my team on field trips to see other developments for themselves to witness the level of quality other developers are producing. Unfortunately, due in part to lack of self-esteem and exposure to good working practices, the concept of taking pride in ones work is foreign to them. To understand the mindset, you have to understand the culture. Coming out of slavery and colonialization, 80 percent of Ghanaians have been raised with the concept of a white God and white superiority. White Jesus is planted all over the country, in churches, schools and on the rear window of vehicles. With that level of indoctrination, it is very difficult for the average Ghanaian to think outside the box. The majority of businesses in Ghana are also owned by Lebanese families, and due to their appearance being of the lighter hue, Ghanaians tend to be timid in nature around such people because of the imposition placed on them.

My team is much more understanding now that I have exposed them to a different level of thought and have encouraged them to always seek what is good and not to accept life sitting down. We regularly have conversations on life, goals, achievements, and regrets. That said, I would never change my experience of moving to Africa, it has by far made me a stronger, zealous individual.

Dirty Games: Land, Real Estate & Renting

Ownership is everything in Ghana. If you plan to buy a property as a second home or you are relocating to Ghana I would advise a few things before making the large step.

1. If you intend to buy land, speak to a person or company that has a proven track record of successful land acquisitions. Take into consideration that land ownership for foreigners is a 50 year lease unless you become a Ghanaian citizen then it's 99 years.

2. Make sure you are ready for a paradigm shift because things do not run on European or American time.

3. Don't come over with the mentality of trying to compare what is outside to what is happening on the ground in Ghana. This country is still battling with the indoctrination of colonialism and a poverty driven mentality.

4. Plan to integrate and not dominate. Ghana is a lovely place once you learn the culture.

5. Familiarize yourself with other returnees/Diasporan who have successfully transitioned into Ghanaian society, emphasis on the word 'successfully'.

6. Be prepared to try new food dishes. Ghana has a wealth of dishes that can make you feel at home. The standard options of KFC, Burger King and Pizza Hut are there too.

7. Don't be too hasty to give money away to charity. Because you see somebody with a need doesn't mean you should be the one to save them. Africa doesn't need charity; it needs good governance and better institutions.

8. Your experience will be totally different from somebody else's so try not to take on other people's negative outlooks towards Ghana. Many have come looking for a husband or wife without first examining their intentions and have been burnt emotionally and financially. In all things, do your due diligence.

Dirty Games: Land, Real Estate & Renting

9. Be prepared for the heat. Ghana is very hot most of the time so please be very careful. Hydrating yourself with water or coconut water is the most natural and refreshing feeling. You will not be disappointed with the supply of drinking water. It is sold practically everywhere including but not limited to the street vendors.

10. And last, don't be too quick to trust anybody, that includes some Diasporan. Not everyone with the same skin complexion as you has the best intentions for you.

After successfully completing my first project, I decided to register a real estate company in Ghana primarily to help those intending to make the transition into Ghana more smoothly without going through the potential headaches I went through initially. Five years in and aiding many individuals and families transitioning into Ghana, Blackwood Property Services Ltd is also available to assist in any property acquisitions. We work with a reputable network of other realtors as well so getting the right advice is never far away. As part of our welcoming Diasporans back home, we hold rooftop events called Akwaaba 360. These events help break the ice and create a soft landing for people transitioning over to Ghana. It also acts as a vehicle to introduce people to the business community over here so don't be afraid to come home. Africa is calling.

 <<<<<<Touch base with Gabriel and contact him for your housing needs in Ghana.

Dirty Games: Land, Real Estate & Renting

Introducing Esi's Paradise

MANAGING TRAFFIC: BUSINESS & INVESTMENT

When I first started driving in Ghana, I quickly realized that driving in Ghana and managing traffic was the perfect analogy for doing business in Ghana. If you have not been to Ghana yet it won't make sense; but if you have, you will surely understand.

There always seems to be a lot of traffic and not every vehicle is road worthy. Many break down in the middle of the road. Trucks are overloaded. Most drivers do not care about any other driver on the road. There are tro-tros (local mini-buses) that drive erratically - willing to risk an accident to pull over and pick up the customer for a 2 cedi ride. There are Okadas (motorbikes) sometimes with 2-3 people without helmets weaving in and out traffic and cutting you off. Taxi drivers doing the same. Everybody is rushing to get their destination at all costs and- sometimes at your expense.

The roads and directions to get to your destination are not always clear, and at any given moment, you may have to go off-road. There are not always clearly delineated lanes and sometimes the street signs are faded. But there are enough Range Rovers, Bentleys, Mercedes, Porsches and Lamborghinis on the road so you're convinced the roads lead somewhere and managing traffic is possible. This for me is what it feels like trying to do and be in business in Ghana – managing traffic.

As you design, create and build your business, I suggest adopting a V8 4x4 type drive which will allow you to sit high enough to see everything around you, comfortable enough to sit in traffic when necessary, powerful enough to carry a load, and versatile enough to a maneuver the sometimes rocky roads and get ahead quickly when the roads are smooth. You must also make sure you can afford the upkeep and repairs to remain in optimal working condition. I believe it's worth it to create a legacy for you family and provide jobs for people who need them.

I often say you don't move to Africa to get a job. You move to Africa to create jobs. The way you create jobs is by creating a business. The opportunity for deep and wide impact is enormous. The opportunity to become wealthy is just as deep, wide and enormous. Those of us who are committed to the soil know this without a doubt. It'll be useless trying to convince us differently. Moreover, I've personally always questioned the serious practice of Pan-Africanism without it being Africa and African-centered--grounded in the idea that returning to the source to reclaim our birthright was the ultimate goal of Pan-Africanism. Empowering Black/African people everywhere starts with empowering Africa.

The potential impact is always as important as the potential to produce wealth. The best way to produce wealth is through low inputs and high outputs scaled exponentially. If your heart is in the right place, you can do very well creating or expanding your legacy while helping others do the same. Sometimes, people just need to know and see what's possible. That alone can encourage them to reach higher and think expansively – well, sometimes. Africa will be developed. The real question is by whom. Beyond sharing and posting stories on social media about how much China and other nations are raping Africa for its raw resources, we need Black people and Black collaboratives more willing to take the risk and do business in and with Africa.

The rest of the world knows Africa is the mother of civilization, center of the world and has remained the next biggest thing forever. Beyond the human labor extracted to build the rest of the world we need to understand the extraction of raw minerals and resources that are fueling the rest of the world's development has never and will never stop. The world cannot exist without Africa. Africa has the youngest population, has the most arable land, space to grow and most recently became the largest free trade zone in the world. She has never relinquished her position as the center of the world. She's deep and vast in her own right outside of we want from or for her.

Africa doesn't need more aid. Africa needs her children to return home and work with their brothers and sisters on the ground to make solid investments and start businesses that help to solve the many problems that exist. Ghana is a great starting point and in all honesty a soft place to land in comparison to many other countries. It is also a great hub for travel and provides the ability to move through the rest of the continent rather smoothly.

Although business and investment in Ghana aren't as clear-cut as some YouTube videos or virtual meetings make it seem, there are so many possibilities to start, partner and/or grow a business in Ghana if you have the bandwidth. It takes a lot of courage, grit, patience, research and perseverance to see it through. Taking your time and leveraging existing relationships and/or giving yourself the time to make sure you have a plan can't be overstated. Even having a solid business plan requires extreme flexibility.

Let's be clear about business as well. You go into business to make a profit. Even if you decide to give away your profit for humanitarian reasons, the purpose of the business is to make profit. If your ultimate why is humanitarianism, you will need that business to make a profit to help others. Regardless of industry or size, for the purpose of this discussion, business is simply the selling of goods or services to make a profit. I am not making a distinction between someone who is investing $5,000 or $500,000 – but if you are coming to Ghana for business, be clear about why you're in business. It can be difficult to remain clear with so much poverty and need around you; however, you have to stay focused. And if you're creative, you can practice compassionate capitalism, make a profit, and still help people.

Managing Traffic: Business & Investment

You have to mind your business. The Ghanaian economy keeps growing every day. Although the government is in support of and welcoming more Diasporans to come to Ghana to set up businesses to help speed up the growth of the economy as well as to reduce the rate of unemployment. While the process of setting up a business can be fairly simple, running and growing the business can be daunting, confusing and frustrating. A mentor once told me unless you have a lawyer, you're not really doing business. When I registered my company in Ghana, I did it through a trusted and recommended lawyer - licensed to practice law in Ghana. And although I run my business daily with local partners, I continually consult my lawyer about the things I want to do and the best way to do them within the confines of the law.

My advice for individuals who want to start a business is to take some time to do your research, work with a trusted local partner (indigenous or expat) and depending on the nature of your business and size of your investment, commit to being on the ground.

Talk to Sam Swift Law Offices>>>>>>>

It's not uncommon to hear stories about people who were cheated and had to start all over so again minding your business is paramount. I don't think a successful business absolutely requires a detailed business plan in the beginning, especially in Ghana; but it helps surely to have a detailed business plan as long as you're flexible to pivot and make adjustments where necessary. For those reading who are new to business in general, please do your research. You can simply google "business plan".

To incorporate a company in Ghana you must do so at the Registrar General's Department and obtain the Certificate of Incorporation and TIN number, Company Regulation and Certificate to commence Business. The forms required are usually

Managing Traffic: Business & Investment

at a small fee and require a fee to submit the forms. Because of the long lines, language barrier and unstable network, this can take a few days. It's great for the experience but time is money. Again, I suggest getting a lawyer to help you complete and file your paperwork. If you're opening your company without a local partner, note that foreign investors are required to comply with the minimum equity requirements which can be either in cash, capital goods relevant to the investment or a combination of both. The minimum foreign equity requirements are:

- US$200,000 for Joint Venture with Ghanaian partner having not less than 10% equity participation

- US$500,000 for 100% foreign ownership

- US$1,000,000 for Trading Activity with a minimum of 20 skilled Ghanaians employed by such an enterprise.

- There is no minimum equity requirement for foreigners interested in the following sectors: manufacturing, export trading and portfolio investment.

- Foreign spouses and Ghanaians with dual nationality are also exempt from the minimum equity requirement.

 <<<<<<<Visit GIPC

You should register with the Ghana Investment Promotion Centre (GIPC) and the Ghana Revenue Authority (GRA) for the purposes of fulfilling statutory tax obligations. Depending on your industry, you may have to register with the Environmental Protection Agency (EPA) or other agencies to comply with their regulatory requirements. Your best source for setting up and registering a business in Ghana is with a lawyer.

There is no one path to creating a successful business in Ghana and no one person or entity who can help you navigate the

Managing Traffic: Business & Investment

sometimes murky waters. There are many reliable and serious people in Ghana who know the market and have the relationships to help you find success. Serious investors and entrepreneurs looking to build a deep and wide legacy of wealth, should work with a trusted agent or partner who is an expert. Finding that person and knowing who to trust can be difficult so I've made it easy.

Amma Gyampo is co-founder of the African B2B Entrepreneurship Advisory and Support firm, ScaleUp Africa. She is also an Advisor to several businesses and strategic bodies including Impact Investing Ghana and women-focused incubator, Kumasi Hive. She is also a thought leader and convener in the Ghanaian Diaspora Business community, Entrepreneurship, Gender Equality and Economic Empowerment ecosystem having been featured in Forbes, BBC and Entrepreneur.com over the years. She recently convened and curated one of the most notable Ghana-Diaspora Business events of 2020, IGNITE.

Introducing Amma Gyampo

For the purposes of this book, it is worth highlighting that ScaleUp Africa periodically conducts group online planning and business development sessions for Diasporans requiring guided support. ScaleUp Africa is currently promoting its Black Entrepreneurship Crowdfund to enable the global Diaspora that wish to give back, an opportunity to support programs and services for the benefit of local youth and women entrepreneurs.

Check out IGNITE Framework for SME Growth and Innovation>>>>>>>>>

Managing Traffic: Business & Investment

Introduction

Having moved to Ghana with a young family almost a decade ago, I'm pleased to share my personal experiences and general advice around business and investment prospects in specific sectors, across Africa as a whole, and Ghana specifically.

Visit Scale Up Africa>>>>>>>>>>>

To say that 2020 was dominated by the COVID-19 pandemic is an understatement; however, it has been a year of resilience, adaptability and new opportunities for entrepreneurs and start-ups across Africa. Within the Tech sector for example, we saw a relatively impressive number of investments estimated at $1.2m for over 420 firms. My firm, ScaleUp Africa is committed to continue building entrepreneurial capacity across corporate, foundation, and diaspora networks with our IGNITE framework as our base curriculum to guide, promote, and increase the level of innovation and small business in Ghana and beyond. We are particularly passionate about Tech, Tourism, Agribusiness and Gender based programs, training, digital solutions and funding with an extensive network of entrepreneurs, business opportunities, and investors across Africa.

General Attitudinal Tips

In the subsequent few segments, I will share a few qualities and sector opportunities to watch out for and incorporate into your plans.

Total Commitment: I moved back to Africa from Europe having reached a stage in my life where I was a burnt out young mother looking for more for my family and my own career prospects. I made a pledge to myself to make this new chapter work no matter what. Our African Adventure had to work no matter what. Settling into life in Ghana has at times been frustrating but I learned quickly to be more empathetic to people's situations locally and not to be overly judgmental about certain situations while preserving and respecting my own time, expectations, and standards. Quite the balancing act - adjusting to the new pace of life around me - the culture, the workforce, the politics of doing business, especially as a woman and as a returnee.

Despite a longer than anticipated period of learning, networking, and building credentials across Africa in the Entrepreneurship Development, Gender Equality and Impact Investment ecosystems, I believe that the following are essential to those in the Diaspora looking to succeed: grit, adaptability, growth mindset and partners that are aligned with your mission and vision.

Culture and Social Networks: Successful African businesses, like most places in the world, are highly dependent upon a robust social culture. In Ghana for example, attendance and support for funerals, engagements and weddings are guaranteed to boost your standing and likelihood of securing deals through such relationships. The more you associate yourself with Associations, Groups and Chambers, the more you will extend your social circles and directly influence your business outcomes.

One thing you will experience and hear often will be requests for 'something small' here and there...the euphemism for little tips and payments. It can be a struggle to understand the fine balance between being a 'big man' or 'big woman' of privilege and status requiring you to display generosity and pure corruption. This is an art rather than a science; however, it is worth noting, seeking counsel, and learning about as you progress through the system. And just like anywhere else in the world, there is, despite the seeming chaos, a system you will need to take time to respect and understand. Failure to do so, will only result in added frustrations and friction that will mostly negatively affect you. My practical message here is to pick your battles very carefully and to know that

Managing Traffic: Business & Investment

there is a deep ethos of dependence, class structures, and related expectations that you will have to navigate.

Playing Politics: If you are going to succeed at scale in business here in Ghana, and wish to secure the level of resources and control for your business and those you serve, you cannot run away from the political cycle and networks that direct opportunities to the business community in Ghana. The higher the level of your political contacts, the better. That's just how it works. However, do exercise the necessary caution and wisdom to hedge against the ever looming political cycles and changes. I leave you with one word: Discretion.

Mass Markets vs Super Niche: Do look at products and services that can serve the mass market, regional or international markets. Many Diasporans start off with niche, lifestyle businesses that remain small. It is worth noting that in the US for example, Black-owned businesses generate on average 25% less revenue due to lack of market access and distribution strategy. In Ghana, having observed many businesses, I cannot advise strongly enough the need to do your homework and look for opportunities to serve the majority and not the few unless you have a super niche solution for a highly specified consumer segment.

Supplier Beware: In an interview with Entrepreneur.com, I share learnings from our baptism of fire in doing business in Africa; our first business entailed supplying wholesale protein products to most of the prestigious hospitality establishments in Ghana. Entrepreneur.com asked 'what I wish I'd known before back then'; my response: 'I wish I'd known what kind of …parameters to apply to the businesses and that I'd been more disciplined with managing cash flow. We had far too many outstanding invoices and big clients that were highly undisciplined with paying invoices on time. However, it was a Catch 22 situation. When you're a new business and you've secured big name clients that are great for prestige, but who are killing you in terms of cash flow, it's difficult to make the right decision for the business – or to even know what that right decision is. We had to learn the hard way that we needed to cut off some big clients that were simply too costly to serve. I also share insights in the interview about managing a team in Ghana.

Check out Entrepreneur.com Article>>>>>>

Hiring & Workforce Management: Making hiring decisions should be based more on character and attitude than apparent skills or experience on a resume. I always advise entrepreneurs doing business in Ghana that you can always teach new technical skills, but you can't teach attitude or character. Some of the employees we have experienced the most stress with, came with an attitude that ultimately brought down and infiltrated the entire team.

We all make mistakes in the early days. Ours included rushing into business initiation and not dealing with toxic staff swiftly enough. Having learnt from these mistakes has only re-affirmed the fact that leaders should never lose their sense of intuition, never be afraid to let toxic staff go, and to look out for character over so-called qualifications or even recommendations. Always utilize probationary periods in your employee contracts, stretch, push and test their abilities to be taught, be managed, and most of all be developed to become prime supporters of your business without too much friction.

Sector Opportunities

Tourism: The Year of Return needs no introduction, having contributed an estimated $1.9m to the Ghanaian economy tapping into the Pan-African and global Black zeitgeist with its new breed of traveler with specific tastes and demands that have emerged to take over the market for tourism services with a preference for experiences which meet specific heritage, sustainability, local community, independence, health & lifestyle needs, for example.

Managing Traffic: Business & Investment

The manner in which tourists will be booking such experiences will continue to change with a growing movement towards direct bookings and more immersive digital marketing efforts emerging from suppliers.

Visit the DANN Residence>>>>>>

In Ghana, we've seen an explosion of experiences riding the wave of the 'ancestry' trend with a growing number of entrepreneurs creating new initiatives, services and travel experiences including Fulani Kitchen's authentic 'Dine On A Mat' concept, breath-taking networking and views at The Agyementl Club House in the Aburi Mountains and Afrocentric, home-like short stays that cater well to the Diaspora traveler such as The DANN Residence in the trendy neighborhood of East Legon.

The Agriculture Business: According to the Food and Agriculture Organisation (FAO) we generate over 1.3 billion tons, one third of the world's total production volume, of food losses and waste post-harvest every single year. Agriculture offers immense opportunities to those in the Diaspora looking to add value across the value chain. From innovative models of investing in Production, to packaging, marketing, logistics, cold chain, and distribution. Whether you chose to fund, produce, process, or market, there are immense opportunities available to take advantage of this growing, dynamic industry. According to the African Development Bank, Africa's Agriculture sector will be worth $1trillion dollars by 2030. For those like myself with an interest in supporting women and making significant strides towards gender equality and Impact, I can't think of a better sector to start in Africa. With the Africa Continental Free Trade Agreement taking effect this year, the Regional and Global Export markets remain an eye watering prospect for those in the Diaspora. In COVID-19 terms, food production is an essential service; if executed properly, with the right business model to mitigate your risk, partnerships, cooling and post-harvest technologies, logistics' solutions, and distribution networks, this sector offers as close as you can get to 'pandemic-proof'.

Do take advantage of local Research and Development resources like CSIR to keep up to date with potential new opportunities from this sector of many value chains and many untapped opportunities for the AfroDiaspora Business community. It goes without saying that Agriculture is highly risky, but highly lucrative if the necessary mitigation measures are put in place from the very start of your endeavors.

Tech: The future of our development is dependent upon capital (financial and human) and technology. The need for extended access to affordable internet particularly in towns, peri-urban and rural areas for Education, Healthcare, Financial Inclusion, Sustainable Development transformation, and even in the field of Agriculture cannot be overstated.

We have already seen entrepreneurs and investors enter the space with the deployment of robots, nanotechnologies, drones for Agriculture and micro sensors for soil and water management, geomapping etc. These are just a few of the examples of potential use cases and investment opportunities in Africa and Ghana specifically that are dependent upon access to affordable internet, infrastructure investments etc. I must emphasize however the amount of cash not just for the Tech and Human Resource, but for Marketing and intense, long-term community and broader stakeholder engagement raises the barrier to entry for any sustainable business in the Tech space.

Export Model: I would like to say a quick word about the potential to generate foreign exchange while operating in Ghana or anywhere else on the continent, if you are able to secure the right buyers and distributors for health, natural, packaging innovations from the Agriculture sector in particular, then you could be onto a winning formula for your start-up.

Closing Tips

In the context of the COVID-19 Pandemic, segments including Health, Financial Services, Water, Sanitation, B2B Logistics and Green Energy all remain attractive opportunities for entrepreneurs from the Diaspora.

In closing, I will share some final tips I often share with our Diaspora start-up clients: Challenge your assumptions and expectations, respect the culture, be flexible, clearly define your supply chain, and a specific off taker or market for your product and finally, start simple and lean with solid partners to mitigate your risk and costs as you embark upon your African venture.

Managing Traffic: Business & Investment

The Gold Coast

I'm often asked about Gold and the mining business since Ghana was once called the Gold Coast. I think Gold is very important for Ghana's sovereignty and in general, mining as well. We are underrepresented, locked out and/or limited to the low end of the value chain. While we don't go too deep here in this chapter, I want to introduce you to Brenda Joyce. I've asked her to share just a little bit about the Gold and Mining business. For those interested, I strongly suggest you connect with Brenda at the end of her contribution.

Introducing Brenda Joyce

Ghana is the number 1 producer of gold on the African continent. It is also number 2 in production of cocoa beans. These are the two major export products of Ghana, and generate millions of dollars of revenue for the Government of Ghana. Although one is Mineral Development and the other is Agriculture or Farming, both are capital intensive and high risk investments, especially for the novice investor. Gold mining, in particular, carries a great deal of risk and attracts elaborate investment schemes where misinformation or partial information is provided the investor, who puts money in but will never see a return or profit on his investment. It's difficult to separate genuine opportunities from fake ones, and extreme caution should be taken when approaching or being offered investment opportunities.

In addition to mining gold, there are several other minerals that can be mined, and precious and semi-precious stones, as well. However the same risks apply. Careful preparation and allowing the time for examination of all relevant information helps protect the investor. Mining is not a 'get rich quick' scheme, but requires significant labor and capital for extensive periods of time.

Managing Traffic: Business & Investment

The mining sector is divided into two sectors, Large-scale mining, and Small-scale mining. Large-scale mining is for major mining companies with experience and knowledge of extractive methods from previous experience. Small-scale mining leases are reserved solely for Ghanaian nationals. The opportunities lie in partnering with these small-scale Ghanaian miners, to provide capital for equipment and upgrading of their sites.

The focus of the Government of Ghana at this time is to add value, called Beneficiation, to their raw materials to increase revenue generation by processing the raw materials into a more finished product before exporting. This would support an increase in the labor base of the country, and increase the revenue generated by exporting finished products rather than the raw materials from which products are made. With the correct examination of data, sufficient capital, and the right Team, mining can be a successful business.

Connect w/ Brenda

Managing Traffic: Business & Investment

Check out the Commemorative Gold
Year of Return Jewelry Collection

DEEPLY ROOTED: TOURISM, CULTURE & ART

"Culture is coded wisdom that has been accumulated for thousands of years and generations. Some of that wisdom is coded in our ceremonies, it is coded in our values, it is coded in our songs, in our dances, in our plays. And because we as a society did not have a written culture, it is not something that we could go back and read about. When our elders died, they died with that culture. And so we were left with a vacuum and we have tried to fill that vacuum with the values that missionaries have given us, but the missionaries have given us values that are based on the bible. And as good as they are, they are not coded wisdom of our people." - **Taking Root: The Vision of Wangari Maathai**

I wholehearted believe that the Year of Return, Ghana 2019 and Beyond the Return will go down in history as the spark that ignited the fire behind one of the most significant and impactful movements centered around connecting the Black diaspora in the 20th and 21st centuries. What's happening with Black people in the Black travel movement doesn't happen without culturally-centered, heritage-focused, and innovative tourism. For most Black people from America, almost all tourism and visits to Africa are heritage tours. Because we've been separated physically from the land, culture, and art of Africa for so long, our ancestral memory is activated and takes over.

<<<<<<Visit the Beyond the Return Site

Tourism plays an important role in our repatriation journey. It helps us thoroughly immerse ourselves with the spirit of the land and connect to the deeply rooted culture and art of our ancestors. Ghana's Tourism landscape is thriving and improving. Beyond the beautiful people and landscapes, there are a plethora experiences across the 16 regions that offer unique cultural encounters and just raw fun, as well. Here are some of the top tourism sites in the most frequently visited regions.

Accra/Greater Accra Region

- **W. E. B. Du Bois Centre** - A memorial place and tourist attraction area that is dedicated to W.E.B Du Bois. The main building is where Dubois lived.
- **Nkrumah Mausoleum** - Mausoleum of the first President of Ghana who led the country to independence and inspired the fight against colonialism
- **Arts Centre** - the biggest arts and crafts centre in Ghana where sculptures, paintings, fabrics among other items are being sold
- **Artists Alliance Gallery** - Biggest art gallery in sub-Saharan Africa
- **Proverbial Casket Shop** - Fantasy or figurative coffins from Ghana
- **Makola Market** - Biggest open air market in Ghana
- **Labadi Beach** - The busiest beach on Ghana's coast
- **Osu Castle** - Also known as Christianborg is a castle located in Osu and was used during the slave trade

Akosombo/Volta Region

- **Shai Hills Forest Reserve** - It's a small, fenced area with interesting wildlife reserve and a wildlife museum
- **Maranatha Island and Volta Estuary** – small island situated just in front of the beach in Ada Foah closer to the estuary.
- **Akosombo Dam** – World's largest man
- **Mount Gemi** – One of the tallest mountains in Ghana
- **Mount Afadja** - it is the third highest mountain in Ghana at 885 m (2,904 ft)

Deeply Rooted: Tourism, Culture and Art

Western Region

- **Nzulezu** – A village entirely made up of stilts and platforms on the water. You can only get there by canoe.
- **Ankasa Forest** - The only area in the Wet Evergreen Forest Zoo
- **Nkroful (Nkrumah Birthplace)** - The hometown of Ghana's first president
- **Bisa Aberwa Museum** - A museum with sculptural representations of wood, clay, cement paintings, and photographs
- **Takoradi Port** - The oldest harbor in Ghana
- **San Antonio Fort** - A Fort built by the Portuguese in 1515 near the town of Axim

Central Region

- **Cape Coast Castle** – Served as a hub for enslaved Africans during the Transatlantic slavery (UNESCO Site)
- **Elmina Castle** - Served as a hub for enslaved Africans during the Transatlantic slavery
- **Kakum National Park** - An exciting canopy walk which suspends about 40m above the forest's ground
- **International Stingless Bee Centre** - This centre shows insight into the life of stingless bees in Africa
- **Crocodile Pond** – Astounding, fascinating and friendly crocodiles you can pet

Eastern Region

- **Aburi Botanical Garden** - Huge botanical garden with lots of trees and flowers. It's a great location for pictures and socialization.
- **Centre for Plant Medicine Research (CPMR)** – Traditional and natural medicine research and growth

- **Tetteh Quarshie Cocoa Farm** - Maiden cocoa farm in Ghana
- **Cocoa Research Institute of Ghana** - Conducts research into the development of by-products of cocoa and other mandate crops
- **Boti Falls** - River Pawnpawn which forms the falls takes it source from Ahenkwa-Amalakpo before falling over an igneous rock
- **Umbrella Rock** - A spectacular rock formation with a great view over the valley discovered by people hiding from t
- **Arboretum Canopy Walk** - The arboretum contains different species of trees and flowers. It has a butterfly sanctuary and a canopy walkway

Northern Region

- **Mole National Park** - Ghana's largest wildlife refuge
- **Paga Crocodile Pond** - A sacred pond which is inhabited by friendly West African crocodiles
- **Larabanga Mosque** - Ghana's oldest mosque and one of the country's most revered religious sites
- **Mystic Stone** - The mystic stone is believed to always return to its exact location when moved
- **Hippopotamus Sanctuary** - A community based initiative that conserves hippopotami and their riparian habitat
- **Kintampo Waterfalls (Brong Ahafo)** - Also known as Sanders Falls during the colonial days is located on the Pumpum river, a tributary of the Black Volta
- **Buabeng Fiema Monkey Sanctuary (Brong Ahafo)** - A monkey sanctuary found between twin communities, Buaben and Fiema
- **Manhyia Palace (Ashanti)** - The home of the overlord or King of the Ashanti Kingdom
- **Okomfo Anokye Sword (Ashanti)** - The immovable sword drive into the ground by Okomfo Anokye

- **Bonwire Kente Shop (Ashanti)** - A town in Ghana where the prestigious cloth in Africa, Kente originated
- **Ntonso Adinkra Home (Ashanti)** - Printing of Adinkra symbols unto a piece of fabric
- **Lake Bosomtwe (Ashanti)** - A lake formed by an ancient meteorite strike. The name means Antelope God because it is said to be discovered by a hunter chasing an antelope that disappeared into the lake.

While my company, The Adinkra Group, facilitates Birthright Journeys which provide an intentional cultural and spiritual reconnection experience, we also offer regional tours and curated journeys for people who want to vacation for a good time.

As a visitor, you get a taste of how culture and art resonates through everyday life as you begin to learn the history, view the architecture, hear and learn to speak the language, dance to the music, eat the food, study the cloth, visit the sites, and immerse yourself. You also begin to learn and see how deeply imbedded many of the cultural traditions are in everyday society - beginning with traditional names, greetings, protocols, and dress. Many tour companies include formal visits with local chiefs where you get to experience a different level of protocol with traditional royalty.

Although there are many cultural groups in Ghana, many are familiar and associate all Ghanaians with the Akan cultural group. Most of us are familiar with kente cloth, Adinkra symbols, Kwame Nkrumah, and Akan day names. Though these are popular cultural elements, they do not represent Ghana's traditions in totality. Each region and cultural group also hosts their own annual festival that's been passed down generationally for hundreds of years. The festivals are normally based around the harvest, purification, or commemoration of a significant historical event. The festivals are not just parties and celebrations, but include a series of spiritual rituals and ceremonies that the people believe are absolutely necessary, and very much tied to their spiritual beliefs and relationship with God. Here's a list of some of the main annual festivals specific to the various cultural groups:

Name	Significance	Group	Region	Date
Homowo	Harvest and Thanksgiving	Ga	Greater Accra	August/September
Hogbetsotso	Commemorating Migration	Anlo	Volta	First Saturday of November
Aboakyir	Religious Festival (live deer hunting)	Effutu (Simpa-Winneba)	Central	First Saturday of May
Bakatue	Fishing Festival	Elmina (Fante)	Central	First Tuesday of July
Kundum	Harvest	Nzema (Ahanta)	Western	August September
Ohum	Purification	Akyem	Eastern	June/July
Adae Kese	Purification	Asante (Akan)	Ashanti	Every six weeks
Asafotufiam	Migration and Harvest	Ada	Eastern	July August
Fetu Afahye	Harvest	Oguaa	Central (Cape Coast)	1st Saturday of September
Odwira	Harvest festival	Akuapem	Eastern	September
Ngmayem	Commemorating migration	Krobos	Eastern	Last Week in October
Akwanbo	Commemorating migration	Gomoa Abora	Central	
Tedudu	Harvest festival	Ho	Volta	September

Deeply Rooted: Tourism, Culture and Art

Connect with our Tour Services>>>>>>>>

Art is everywhere in Ghana but there are intentional spaces and galleries that showcase Ghana's love and commitment to art. Here is a list of some of the top art galleries in Ghana.

- Arts Centre (Centre for National Culture)
- Art Without Borders Gallery
- Nubuke Foundation
- ANO
- Kuenyehia
- National Museum of Ghana
- The Ark Gallery
- Gallery 1957
- Tiga African Art Consultancy
- The Loom
- Artists' Alliance Gallery
- Berj Art Gallery
- Nanoff Gallery

 <<<<<<Connect with the Art Galleries

Moreover, Art has been one of the primary vehicles for telling stories and safeguarding Ghanaian culture and history. It has the power to describe a nation and its people without a single word or utterance. It collectively builds a wall around culture, keeping it protected from those who might want to change, dilute, or interpret it for a purpose counterproductive to its own existence.

When cobwebs unite, they can tie up a lion. ~ African Proverb

Deeply Rooted: Tourism, Culture and Art

Join the Adinkra Cultural Arts Studio

ENDLESS ENJOYMENT: NIGHTLIFE & ENTERTAINMENT

If there is one area where social media posts about Ghana are as close to accurate as social media can be, it's nightlife and entertainment. I firmly believe that Ghana is one of the top three enjoyment capitals of the world. As the title of this chapter suggests, Ghanaian nightlife and entertainment are endless enjoyment. To be more specific, Accra is the enjoyment capital but enjoyment is everywhere in Ghana. If you're lucky you can start and end your night at Republic Bar & Grill

Connect with Republic >>>>>>>>>>

The nightlife culture in Accra is quite vibrant and often livelier than most urban centers. From table reservations to bottle service, VIP sections and celebrity appearances, there is a universal nightlife culture, The public-facing events and parties we see on social media are an extension of private house parties, private WhatsApp and text groups, brand launches, weddings, birthday parties, private dinners, brunches, football games (soccer), business coalitions and funerals that underscore the authenticity and connectedness you feel as an outsider looking in.

Ghana was already a center of enjoyment prior to the Year of Return. Despite rampant poverty, when it's time to stop work, get dressed, and enjoy, Ghanaians know how to enjoy at every level. There seems to be a natural alignment with the spirit of enjoyment and a work-life balance. Whether you are in a roadside dive bar with no modern luxuries or on a 25 floor rooftop sipping the finest champagne with the city landscape as backdrop, the raw spirit of enjoyment is present.

Endless Enjoyment: Nightlife & Entertainment

There is no time of the year where Ghanaian nightlife is boring. Depending on your budget and relationships, you can have access to the most exclusive parties with the Ghanaian "in crowd", which can be a bit reserved, or with the general population where pleasure is without reservation. Friday night is the top enjoyment night. Saturday night is too close to church on Sunday morning and Ghana nights are not proper unless you hear the rooster crow, the sun is up, and you're eating Rockz Waakye for breakfast.

Eat Rockz Waakye>>>>>>>>

While nightlife is exciting all year round, Easter and Christmas are the apexes of fun in Ghana. This is when the biggest events are hosted and nightlife is incredibly insane. Easter and Christmas are when Ghanaians abroad come home to visit their family and friends. Many save all year long to ensure that when they come home, the budget stays open and the pleasure is unlimited. African Americans starting to flock in large numbers are actually joining a long-standing December in Ghana tradition.

<<<Follow Afrochella for December Enjoyment

When you visit Ghana and experience the nightlife the right way, it's incredible. Likewise, experiencing it the wrong way can be extremely frustrating and it's not enjoyable. Standing in long lines, arriving too early, traveling the wrong route and getting stuck in traffic, breaking the dress code, and just not having an understanding of the flow of the nightlife, are examples of the wrong way. A night that proceeds smoothly without incident, hassle, or inconvenience with reserved seats and or tables, is the right way for maximum enjoyment.

When you live in Ghana, nightlife becomes a bit different. It's easy to get caught in the allure of Ghanaian nightlife because the vibes

Endless Enjoyment: Nightlife & Entertainment

and energy are so high it feels like you can do it every weekday and weekend. Living in Accra, you have different choices to make. Nightlife can serve you well to provide the much needed relief from the week or connect you with the right people; or it can also be the biggest distraction supporting a lack of focus for why you're there, or leave you with no money, and packing up to move back faster than you'd expect. However, if you are interested in the nightlife or entertainment industry, Ghana has a booming market that is ripe for new ideas, venues and concepts. Osu is the party center of Accra.

Enjoyment should be embraced with safety and attention to your surroundings. While there isn't a lot of crime in Accra, people lose their phones or get them stolen, get pick-pocketed, and robbed when they are not paying attention. Women should remain cognizant, aware, and careful with who they meet and accept drinks from to avoid being drugged and sexually assaulted. There are sick people everywhere unfortunately. Driving intoxicated is a mistake everywhere you go but it's more deadly when the roads sometimes have large potholes and the streets are inadequately lit. You should also be careful and focused to prevent police shakedowns and intimidation. Many of the same dangers that exist in America when out enjoying the night in urban settings exist in Ghana, with the exception of gun violence.

Some of my favorite Nightlife Spots >>>>>>>>

The entertainment industry in Ghana is a developing global force. As much as Ghanaians love, emulate, and integrate Black American popular culture into their own, they love their own culture and have a lot of pride in all things Ghanaian. The music business in Ghana is quickly emerging as Ghana has its own Afrobeat(s) stars. To the novice, most things Afrobeat(s) come out of Nigeria but to the more familiar ear, Ghana has its own industry and artists who are taking the world by storm and making their mark. Live performances by the

Endless Enjoyment: Nightlife & Entertainment

major artists are always packed. While there aren't many dedicated concert halls, (which is an enormous opportunity for an entertainment investor) parks, conference centers, beaches, and open fields are easily transformed into entertainment venues.

The film industry in Ghana is not as progressive as the music business, but it's rising. Nollywood strictly refers to the Nigerian film machine, although many people credit all African movies to Nollywood. It desperately needs more resources and support from government and the private sector to grow. The talent is available. There is an enormous opportunity for the right investor to build a modern, professional movie studio in line with international standards.

I can't talk about entertainment without talking about social media influencers who have become an important part of the daily entertainment fabric. Their individual and collective voices help to influence how the industry moves. They're also responsible for attracting more African American influencers, artists and potential investors to Ghana. They expose the world to Ghanaian popular culture. Their potential to elevate Ghanaian brands and help them gain international recognition is ripe.

I am clear that repatriating with a focus on cultural and ancestral connections is not just about spiritual journeys and reconnecting with your ancestral roots. We get to enjoy the totality of who we are without justification or explanation. For the sensitive and consciously aware, it may take some time to be ok with this. We can pour libation for the ancestors and pop bottles for the living. It all goes together.

Follow Ghanaian Entertainment Sites>>>>>>>

MEDIA & MESSAGING

Until the lions have their own historians, the history of the hunt will always glorify the hunter." – **African Proverb**

Media and messaging are powerful tools. We've seen more vividly throughout the past few years how cell phone footage of police murdering innocent Back people and social media reports of white supremacy, have brought wider-spread awareness of racial injustice. We've seen how social media has become a tool for marginalized citizens to tell their own stories and altered long-held, often false narratives around who they are. We've seen how media and messaging was used – even by the highest office in the US, to incite riots, create violence, and reinforce inaccurate stereotypes and racial tropes.

The Year of Return also used media and messaging to tell the world a different story about Ghana. An intentional strategy was put into place to show the world that Ghana is a beautiful, safe, and diverse destination capable of managing large groups of people from the diaspora seeking to connect with their roots. This publicity sparked a movement for media outlets from around the world to pursue stories about what was driving people to Ghana. The end result was a plethora of free marketing for Ghana.

The history of Ghanaian public and private media is directly aligned with its leadership power struggles from the time Ghana became independent in 1957 through the development of its current constitution in 1992. Malcolm X once said, "The media's the most powerful entity on earth. They have the power to make the innocent guilty and to make the guilty innocent, and that's power. Because they control the minds of the masses." In fact, it was the surge of independent press towards the end of colonial rule promulgating self-reliance and freedom that helped lead Ghana to independence from the British in 1957.

Media & Messaging

Kwame Nkrumah himself controlled most of the media although I purposely believe his push for sovereignty, self-reliance and national unity was as good a cause as any. He understood the power of media and messaging in pushing Ghana towards self-reliance. "Free speech" didn't really exist in Ghana until after the 1992 constitution and many still question it's authentic existence today because media is sometimes silenced when their editorials and stories are not in favor of the state.

The Ghana Broadcasting Corporation (GBC) is the state-owned TV and radio outlet. Television was introduced in 1965 and remained state-owned until 1994. FM radio began in 1988. The Daily Graphic and Ghanaian Times are state-owned publications, but the Daily Graphic is the only truly nationally-distributed newspaper. There are a number of other independent newspapers and daily periodicals but national distribution remains a challenge. There is an opportunity here. Most of the state papers publish propaganda in favor of government that encourage support for their policies and remain conservative in nature. Other private independent or opposition papers are normally publicizing government editorials and articles questioning government management decisions and the latest government scandal. Free media as we know it is relatively new in Ghana.

As you become a resident and citizen, you'll find out the media content broadcast in Ghana is a bit different than the media content used to advertise Ghana to the rest if the world. While there is some native Ghanaian content, most of the media content on television comes from South Africa, India, and Europe. This programming rarely promotes progressive, culturally affirming content.

Most radio and TV news is delivered in a mixture of Twi and English, or another local language depending on coverage area, so it can be difficult to follow for those who only speak English.

Media & Messaging

Radio music and entertainment is much more diverse. While Ghanaian music and afrobeat run the airwaves, there's a great deal of reggae, hip hop, and new and old R&B programming, as well.

The bulk of the traditional and contemporary media space is dominated by coverage of Ghanaian celebrities, artists, socialites, the wealthy and frequent reports on local scandals and the activities of politicians. With the exception of very large International stories – like US elections and the murder of George Floyd, most of the news coverage is limited to Ghanaian affairs. One can always subscribe to international news outlets via cable television – DSTV is the most popular – to have access to CNN, BBC, Al Jazeera, and other international news channels.

The process of engaging print media for the purposes of public relations and to create a digital footprint is very different from what happens in the US. In Ghana, if you want the media to cover a story, you will need to pay a journalist. Though the cost is fairly nominal – a small fee to cover transportation, meals, and a small retainer for the staff – this is a necessity for written news coverage. If you need a publicist or media services in Ghana, I trust and recommend Wax Print Media.

<<<<<<<<Connect with WaxPrint Media

Many Ghanaian print media companies don't have vehicular capacity for their field journalists, and simply can't afford to send their staff out on assignment. Radio and TV media are a bit more like the US. You can have your publicist pitch the story and if they like it and it aligns, you'll be on radio and TV. However, nothing trumps having great relationships with on-air personalities or show producers. There is an enormous opportunity in the media space in Ghana for entrepreneurs in the radio, TV and print news industry as well as for content creators.

Media & Messaging

My next guest contributor, Ivy Prosper, is a media professional in Ghana and blossoming content creator, writer and TV News Anchor. Here, she shares her experiences and advice working in the Ghanaian media sector.

Introducing Ivy Prosper >>>>>>>>>>>>

If you're reading this, it means you are seriously considering making a move or investing in Ghana. The transition is not an easy one, and it's good you've taken the time to research your options and learn from others who have done it before you. There are so many lessons to be learned and you will also have your own learning curve that will become your teacher in Ghana. It's taken a lot for me to make it this far and trust me when I say, the journey still has its challenges every day. Ghana is no walk in the park and you have to prepare yourself, mind, body and soul for the experience.

Ghana is in an exciting time as the nation continues to experience a renaissance. It's a country that has long been known for its Pan-Africanism and has attracted so many people from the global African diaspora since the country's independence. At the foundation of Ghana's birth is the desire to reconnect with her brothers and sisters from around the world. The nation's first President, Dr. Kwame Nkrumah extended the invitation to the Black diaspora from the start. With the likes of Dr. Martin Luther King Jr., Malcolm X, and Muhammad Ali, having made the journey to Ghana, it was the beginnings of what we see today.

It's not only high profile people who have heeded the call to reconnect with the motherland, but countless others who have started new chapters of their lives in Ghana and other parts of the African continent. In September 2018, Ghana's President Nana Akufo-Addo, announced the official launch of the 'Year of Return 2019' campaign. This campaign was marking the 400 year anniversary of the documented ship of enslaved Africans that

Media & Messaging

arrived in Virginia on August 20, 1619. In commemorating this date, Ghana invited African Americans to make the journey to visit Ghana during the 'Year of Return'. Within a short time, the government recognized the importance of including all people from the global Black diaspora communities. People from the Caribbean, Canada, South America were all feeling the connection to the history tied to the trans-Atlantic Slave trade and wanted to make the journey home to the motherland. The result was one of the most phenomenal years in Ghana's history.

Follow Beyond the Return on Instagram>>>>

At the time of this writing, I am currently working as the Social Media Manager for **'Beyond the Return' and the 'Year of Return'** under Ghana Tourism Authority. This role put me in a position where I was at the forefront of communicating with the diaspora community through our social media platforms. I was and continue to curate content that would be shared with the world. I quickly learned through messages in our inbox, how so many people were longing to come to Ghana. Some fueled by the never-ending racism experienced where they lived, others seeing opportunities for business and to work in a landscape where the people around look just like them. There's something special about feeling a sense of belonging and that's what most people would feel when they came to Ghana.

Before the 'Year of Return' in 2019, there was already a movement of young people of African descent in their twenties and thirties making the move to Ghana. The likes of Producer, Nicole Amarteifio and Actor/Producer Ama K. Abebrese left their lives in the United States and the United Kingdom respectively, to pursue new opportunities in Ghana to create. Amarteifio, is the creator of 'An African City', which was a successful series that followed the lives of five single women in Ghana who had moved back home from abroad. It was a storyline nobody had seen before coming out

Media & Messaging

of Africa. Some questioned its validity, but it resonated with so many people in the diaspora who saw it as similar to lifestyles they had in their own countries. It broke the stereotypes of what it's like to live in a metropolitan African city. Abebrese, who worked as an actress in the U.K., knew that coming to Ghana would be a great way to work in an environment where opportunities were not lost because of being a Black woman, which can be an obstacle in other countries. Since moving to Ghana she's now one of the most successful in the media industry.

A lot of people I meet think that I moved to Ghana because of the 'Year of Return' activities and the call for the diaspora to come home. I was living in Ghana between 2011 - 2013, years before the campaign. During that time I worked at a private secondary school and eventually was hired to host and be the reporter on the Maternal Health Channel TV Series. My initial trip was never planned to be a move. It was supposed to simply be a getaway, but through socializing and networking it quickly turned into career opportunities presenting themselves to me.

I never imagined that one day I would be living in Ghana. The truth is, Ghana was never on my radar. It was always the place of my birth, the place of my heritage and a place I could go visit family, but not a place I wanted to live. There are days when I even think to myself, "Wow, I can't believe I'm living in Ghana." My dream was always to live in New York City. Make it big in the fashion business or be a big time Talk Show Host with my own show or co-hosting on 'The Today Show'. Today my focus has shifted towards being somewhere I can make a significant impact for the continent of Africa.

The beauty of working in the media landscape in Ghana is that it's an area that has so much untapped potential. It's a work in progress where you can get your feet wet, and create something from nothing. Although I have spoken more about film and television, working in the media industry also includes advertising, radio, digital media, newspapers and magazines. There's opportunity to dive into any of these areas.

People who don't understand that Ghana and Nigeria have their own industries, would lump them together under the 'Nollywood' banner. Although many Ghanaians and Nigerians are known to work together on various film projects, they have separate industries. Nollywood has become a power player in film production and continues to produce content so quickly it's like a manufacturing plant for film. Despite the popularity of Ghanaian films among African and Caribbean communities in places like New York, London and Toronto, the industry doesn't have as much financial stability as it does in Nigeria. The film and television industry in Ghana has opportunities for growth especially with more people from the diaspora coming to create content and share stories with the world.

If you're interested in coming to Ghana to be a part of the media industry, you must prepare to enter a landscape that may not be as simple as where you came from. The logistics of doing a project in Ghana can have its challenges. When international companies come to film documentaries or feature film projects, they always come prepared with all their own equipment. Access to the tools necessary for your productions are not always readily available. Filmmakers, Directors, and Photographers are always challenged with staying up to date with the latest equipment. Shipping costs to Ghana can be astronomical, with the port charging duties that are sometimes up to 50% of the value of the equipment being shipped. This is largely the reason that many choose to ask friends, family and colleagues to bring items on flights to avoid the challenge at the port.

The Black Star Film Festival was launched by Juliet Yaa Asante in 2015 as a way to bridge the gap between the African film industry and the global movie industry. The festival focuses on the business side of filmmaking through the workshops and panel discussions that take place throughout the annual festival. It takes place in August every year and is a great way to network and meet people who could potentially become resources for doing work.

My first foray into the industry in Ghana was as the Host and Reporter on The Maternal Health Channel Television Series I mentioned earlier. It was produced by a local production company and aired on two different television stations. The show was a success and reached audiences across the country as we shared knowledge and information on the state of maternal health in Ghana. It was one of the most rewarding and exciting productions I've ever worked on. The project was funded by foreign money, which is often the case when looking to do high-budget projects in Ghana.

Access to funds and the tools to do the work necessary in the film and television industry is one of the biggest obstacles. With less funding, this means everyone on the project would be paid according to the budget. It's important that you know working in Ghanaian media may mean taking a significant salary cut. This can be averted if you choose to start your own production and seek out foreign funding or sponsorship for your projects.

The salary I received as the host and reporter on the television series was considered to be high in Ghana. At the time, I didn't know that and it gave me a false impression of what kind of money could be made working in the television industry in Ghana. It wasn't until in 2016, when I came back to Ghana after a few years later, that I got the reality check about salary expectations. I was very shocked learning about the low rates some people on-air were receiving relative to what someone in the same position elsewhere could potentially be making.

Media & Messaging

I also had the opportunity to work as a Producer in a documentary film with a production company that largely worked with clients who were in the United States. Because of the budgets from the clients, it was an opportunity to earn a better wage than with other locally based companies. I loved that position because it was wonderful to be a part of something that was sharing indigenous stories about food, culture, tradition and human rights in African countries. This was doing work that also served a greater purpose.

Most on-air talent in Ghana are not earning the big salaries you would hear about in the U.S., U.K., Canada and other parts of the developed world. This is why it's important to obtain endorsement deals, and do work that allows for multiple streams of income. This isn't exclusive to the media landscape in Ghana. A lot of people find themselves doing multiple things in other career choices, so that they too have various streams of income.

If your intention is to come to Ghana as a journalist, writer, reporter, filmmaker, or producer, be prepared to network in order to make the right connections and get your foot in the door. Like anywhere else in the world, who you know plays a big role in the opportunities being presented to you. It's also important to note that if you need to make a certain income level to support a lifestyle you want to maintain, it's critical that you also seek out opportunities that are outside the country while living in Ghana. It's not enough to secure a full-time position at a television station or with a production house.

Making the decision to come to Ghana and work in the media is a right one because we are in a time when Africans are telling their own stories. Africans want to take control of their narrative and we are seeing that through social media platforms - YouTube, Instagram, Facebook. Your talent and advantage of being positioned on the ground, gives you the opportunity to pitch stories to productions abroad. For example, both BBC and CNN have

Media & Messaging

people in Ghana who create stories that are shared for their platforms.

Understanding how people communicate in Ghana is important when writing stories or editing pieces. You have to decide if your desire is to create content for Ghanaians and Africans or if you're trying to serve the masses outside of the continent. This will dictate how you operate and navigate the landscape. For example, I've learned so many different things about how the British speak English since moving to Ghana because Ghanaians use British English. In Canada, much of how we communicate is similar to the United States, at the same time we do have some ways of spelling things the British way. So it was a learning curve for me in the beginning. It's important to learn how things are done so that you're as successful as possible when working in the media business.

The industry is one that has its ways of being a little behind in its systems at times. This shows there is room for growth and opportunities for you. Obstacles become teaching moments and it's important not to be condescending towards people when you're bringing ideas to the table.

One important part of your decision to move to Ghana and work in the media space is purpose. I strongly believe that choosing to come to Ghana and work in an industry where the financial reward may not be as great as you would have in your home country, requires that you have a true purpose in what you're doing. Many people I meet are looking to make an impact in the world through their work. What better way to do that than helping to share stories from the continent through the media. Whether it's documentary, images, books, news or film; giving a new perspective and breaking the stereotypes is the key to succeeding.

V8 VS. EVERYBODY: TRANSPORTATION

Planning how you will get around in Ghana ahead of your arrival will be important. If you aren't shipping a car or purchasing a car in Ghana – there are several public transportation options. The main forms of public transportation in Ghana are tro-tro (public van), taxi cabs, Okadas (motorbikes), shared ride companies (Uber and Bolt), bicycles or walking. If public transportation is your form of transport, access to reliable forms of it should be considered when you choose where you will live.

Tro-tros are independently owned, 12 – 15 passenger vans that run local and short distance routes from one station to another. A tro-tro is operated by two people, the driver and the assistant. The assistant normally sits behind the front passenger seat and is responsible for collecting money, advertising the route by through the use of hand signals out the window, and yelling the route which is inaudible to the untrained ear. Tro-tros can take some time to figure out, as there is no signage on the vehicle indicating a final destination and most operators don't speak English. The drivers move very quickly from stop to stop, and the pace can feel quite harried unless you're at the station of origin waiting for passengers to fill the seats.

All tro-tros start and end at a tro-tro station, where vans are lined up in order of arrival and divided between those with air conditioning and those without. There is normally a sign on the top of the van that lists the main areas or stops between the start and end of the route. The tro-tros don't leave the station until each is filled to capacity - normally 14 people. You can wait hours for a tro-tro to depart if you're one of the first to arrive.

When you see tro-tros on the street, they're moving pretty quickly. Depending on the time of day, express tro-tros are available. These vans make fewer stops until they arrive at a certain location.

V8 vs. Everybody: Transportation

And when they stop, they fill up quick because there are many people waiting. Tro-tros are not always very comfortable, and depending on your movement for the day, you could start off early and still end up arriving to your destination late. As mentioned earlier, tro-tros are filled to capacity so it's not odd for someone to ask you to hold their baby or bag. People are very communal in that way and it's not a problem. The good thing is you learn your route and the city very quickly. You will also meet people and likely make friends because you'll need to ask questions to make sure you're on the right track. Tro-tros are the least expensive form of transportation and run all day beginning about 5:30 am until about 10 pm but that varies.

If you're traveling long distances on the tro tro, you can purchase the two or three seats next to you if you require more space or want to stretch out. This is going to really feel privileged and it is. But it's the only way to get a more comfortable ride if that's what you require but want to keep a low budget.

I'm sure I have some trauma regarding taxi drivers that I brought with me to Ghana. I had to spend many nights walking home in DC because taxi drivers wouldn't pick up Black people. I don't like taxi drivers because of this but I've met some good taxi drivers who are fair and reliable. In Ghana, taxis are also mostly privately owned and the driver is normally leasing the taxi. Taxi drivers have a set fee to pay the owner at the end of the week or month, so their primary focus is their daily quota. Some taxis are available for private hire for longer distances. Others traveling short distances are available for shared rides.

Taxis drivers are not always knowledgeable about the exact place you're going so it's useful to learn the general area and some landmarks. There is a big difference between saying, "I'm going to Osu" and, "I am going to Osu by the Papaye". Knowing landmarks can save you a headache, time, and a possible argument about the price because the driver went the wrong way, got lost, or stuck

V8 vs. Everybody: Transportation

in traffic. There aren't taxi meters and a common price structure, so your final price is based on your negotiation skills.

Many taxi drivers will raise the price the moment they hear your accent. Whatever price they say, you want to immediately respond with confidence that it's too much. The next response is normally, "how much will you pay?" At that point you can take off 5 or 10 cedis. No taxi driver will take less than he can afford to take so do not worry about being unfair to the driver, they won't allow it. Make sure you agree to a price before the ride to avoid a disagreement once you've arrived.

Okadas (motorbikes) are normally the quickest and can be the least expensive form of transportation. They are also generally the least safe form of transportation. Many drivers cut in and out traffic, drive against traffic and drive between lanes. Many also don't have helmets for their passengers. Okada drivers can be a nuisance to cars and trucks because it's difficult to see them and they rarely follow road rules.

Uber and Bolt are the primary ride sharing apps available in Ghana. The great thing about Uber and Bolt is they work as they are intended for the most part. They will come to pick you up and drop you off at your location, although sometimes finding the locations can be a challenge. Many drivers will also call you after they accept the trip and ask you where you're located and where you're going. This is either because they don't want to turn their data on or the network is bad. But if you're going to a place where they don't think they'll be pinged for another ride, they'll ask you to cancel the trip or cancel it themselves. The price is normally better than a taxi. Uber and Bolt are readily available within Accra, Greater Accra and Kumasi, but you won't find them in many other areas. The downside to Uber and Bolt is that many drivers are not proficient in reading their GPS and the network isn't always reliable - preventing their app from operating optimally.

V8 vs. Everybody: Transportation

I learned from an Uber driver that drivers will cancel your trip if they see you are paying with a credit card because it takes too long for them to get paid. One thing you can do to avoid this and get a better request/accept ride ratio is to set up an uber cash account once you get your local number, and use a local name like Kwabena or Abena. You'll find the reception is generally a bit different but they may also start speaking in Twi.

If you're going to invest in a vehicle and have the means, the V8 SUV is the king of the road in Ghana – for several reasons. Because you sit fairly high up, you're able to see all your surroundings clearer and can avoid accidents. You have more seats to carry more people and cargo. V8 4x4 SUVs are normally built strong and can endure a lot of wear and tear, which you will experience on the roads. Ghana traffic is aggressive and most people are not friendly drivers. It always feels like a competition for how many people you can pass, not let over, and not let in traffic but it's hard to resist or bully a larger truck.

Large trucks handle bad road conditions and rain much better. As long as they are in good condition, they have fairly good advantages. It's also assumed that only "big men" or "big women" own V8's because most ministers, government officials and "important people" drive V8s. This has benefits at the police stops and often times reserved parking spaces will be opened for you. The downfall is that gas, repairs and maintenance are going to be more costly than with smaller vehicles. Additionally, if you're shipping your own V8, the duty will cost you more than the average vehicle due to the vehicle's weight. Despite how reckless tro-tro drivers, taxi drivers and Okadas are on the road, they are the backbone of Ghana's transportation system and most people rely heavily on them.

Transportation services in Ghana>>>>

SHIPPING, MOVING & LIVING

Repatriating doesn't mean you have to start all over. It can actually be less expensive to bring necessary items with you on your move. You may also find that some household goods from the US are superior in quality and construction – and may be difficult to source an equivalent version in Ghana. However, if you're up for a completely new experience, feel free to simply bring yourself and your bags!

Shipping

Shipping your items to Ghana doesn't have to be difficult, but it does take some planning. There are two main ports in Ghana, both overseen by the Ghana Ports and Harbour Authority (GPHA). One is in Tema, near Accra, and the other in Takoradi, on the west end of Ghana. Depending on where you plan to live, the port you choose to ship your items will make a difference. Many people will want to ship their items to Tema as most people move closer to Accra. However, if you're moving to Cape Coast or farther west, near Takoradi, you may want to ship your items there.

Shipping by boat is the most affordable option as using an air courier is cost prohibitive for most people. Shipping by boat requires your items be stored in a containers which come in sizes of 20 feet (half container) and 40 feet (full container) sizes. The cost ranges from $2000 - $5000 respectively. If you're in the Midwest or on the west coast of the US, you will need to arrange to have your items shipped to the east coast, as this is where most of the ports are located. This will increase your total shipping cost.

Before choosing a shipping company, you will need to determine what you will bring. The best approach is to make a list of everything you think you may need. Once you have that list, begin to sell or give away the items that didn't make the list. After you've scaled down to the items on your list, go through that list again and

Shipping, Moving and Living

shrink it as much as possible. If the house you are renting or purchasing is furnished, you won't need to bring as much.

The most essential items are living, dining and bedroom furniture (if renting an unfurnished or semi-furnished home); essential electronics, bookshelves and books; kitchenware; artwork; clothing; bedding; window treatments, and a car. I don't suggest bringing any kitchen appliances, major or countertop as you will have to make sure they are all connected to a step down converter to change the electric current or they'll get burned out. Be as detailed as possible with your list and have an idea of the value of items you're shipping. If possible, create a spreadsheet so you can easily edit and update it. This will eventually become the manifest you provide to your agent that will help them provide you with a duty quote.

Once you have a list, you want to find a qualified agent with experience connected to the port in the States and who has a partner in Ghana they work with to clear your items. You can and should take time to vet these companies and compare their prices. Beyond the cost of the container rental to ship your items, you will also be responsible for paying the duty on your items. That manifest will help them determine the duty that will be assessed on which items.

If you are shipping a car or truck, the cost depends on number of items. Note that Ghana does not allow cars over 10 years old so if you ship in 2021, the car can't be manufactured before 2011. Salvaged vehicles are also no longer permitted. The duty on the car or truck will depend on the country of origin, make, model, year, and engine capacity. Engine sizes of 2950 cubic centimeters or higher are considered luxury vehicles and will have a higher duty. They are also subject to respective levies. The duty on each vehicle varies but tractors, bulldozers, ambulances, commercial vehicles that have the capacity to transport more than ten persons,

Shipping, Moving and Living

and commercial vehicles for the transportation of goods are exempt.

Once you've selected your shipping company, work with them to approximate the arrival time of your container. Most shipping companies will provide a tracking number for your shipment. You should plan to arrive in Ghana at least a month or a few weeks before your container. When your container arrives, the clearing agent will allow you to come inside the port to witness the cutting of the seal on your container and watch them unload it. All of the items are unloaded and the clearing agents work with port authorities to inspect, tally the duty, and clear everything before you are allowed to leave the port. To help things flow smoother, make sure your agent has the requested amount of money for duty and clearing by the time the container arrives. While it's useful to be there, observe, and ask questions, stay out the way and let them do their job. A good clearing agent will have several people working with them, with the capacity to clear your goods in one day. They will hire one of the trucks on site to transport all your goods to your new home.

If you are shipping items in individual barrels instead of half or full container, you will still need a manifest. Barrels are easier to be picked up and when they arrive, your clearing agent will call you and have you them pick them up from the warehouse.

There is a very important step that I learned the hard way. If you are shipping your items and have included yourself as the receiver, it would be wise to get your residency and Tax Identification Number (TIN) before your trip to receive your container. You will need these and residency permit to clear the items before you go to the port to collect your items. If you are shipping to a different receiver, they will have to do it for you. It was important to ship my container to myself and go through every step of the process myself so I can have full understanding of the process.

Shipping, Moving and Living

When you land at the airport on the trip that you will receive your items from the port, you must stop at Customs in the Arrival Hall before you depart the airport or within 48 hours to pick up a Passengers Unaccompanied Baggage Declaration (PUBD). This form is required for passengers who have sent personal effects in advance or are expecting personal effects after their arrival for declaration.

The PUBD has to have a number of signatures before you can go to the port to receive your container. If you get the form on arrival or within 48 hours, it's complimentary and the process can be much simpler. If not, you will have pay for the form and go through a long drawn out process at the Airport Customs Division which is outside the airport but right next door. Make sure you discuss this form and process with your shipper.

<<<<<<<More about the PUBD and Customs through the Ghana Revenue Authority (GRA)

Moving

In the weeks before your container arrives, use this time to inspect your house or apartment. Ensure that it is clean, painted, and in the condition promised in your negotiations. I suggest you arrive at least a month before your container. The individuals hired to load your items at the port and unload at your home, are not required to provide full move-in, unpacking services. Before you and your items leave the port, you will need to have a conversation with your clearing agent and agree to a price for any hired hands who will help you move in, (i.e. move the larger items to the room they belong).

Arriving in advance also gives you the opportunity to do a few things that will make moving in and living a much smoother transition. This includes turning on your utilities and finding the

Shipping, Moving and Living

closest utility branches to your home. The Electric Company of Ghana (ECG) offers either prepaid electricity where you add money to your meter through their app or a local store; or an ECG card that you have to take to a certified ECG dealer, have them add funds to the card and then tap the card physically against the electric meter to sync your credit.

Arriving early also allows you to get to know your neighborhood and neighbors. Go walking in the morning and early evening. Visit the shops in your neighborhood. Learn the streets and watch the traffic patterns. Find your preferred grocery store, cleaners, bank, and/or carwash. Find your neighborhood bars and restaurants. Find a tailor near you. Make sure you have your MTN broadband internet installed at your house and you don't have any issues. Find your local phone store. Identify the Forex exchange bureaus near you.

Once your container is cleared, you should be prepared to move in. We know the best laid plans often go awry so be sure to build in a safeguard. Having gone through the process and having a great relationship with both our shipper out of Maryland and the agent in Ghana, we can help you through this process.

 <<<<<Connect about shipping and moving

Living

You do have to pay taxes in Ghana and it's important to have an understanding of where you have to pay taxes and how. There are a number of taxes in Ghana including the following:

- Withholding Tax
- Corporate Income Tax

Shipping, Moving and Living

- Mineral Royalty Tax
- Gift Tax
- Vehicle Tax
- Rent Tax
- Income Tax

I am not an expert on Taxes in Ghana so as I've suggested earlier, you should consult a lawyer and/or a trusted and recommended CPA on the ground in Ghana who understands Ghana's Tax laws and processes. However, you should educate yourself as much as possible on taxes in Ghana. The best place for you to learn the basics is through the Ghana Revenue Authority (GRA).

Visit the GRA Tax Site>>>>>>>>>>

Most of the daily Ghanaian living technicalities we've covered in the previous sections. The rest you'll figure out on your own. You'll figure out what works for you and what doesn't work for you across the board. I do believe it's important to have up close and personal experiences of your own. Experience will truly be the best teacher in some instances. Others - I pray you never have to experience. The main tool you need for living in Ghana is patience. It will be important to pack your patience every day, be willing to adjust and pivot at moment's notice when necessary.

Akwaaba!

Thank You

Kwame Nkrumah, first President of Ghana said "I am not an African because I was born in Africa but because Africa was born in me."

We believe the empowerment of African people in the Diaspora requires a connection with Africa. Our mission is to help African people globally, establish a direct connection with Africa to celebrate and build upon our shared ancestral heritage through art, education, cultural immersion, and small business development and investment.

We celebrate our resilience and help make connections that provide a reciprocal exchange to eliminate the stereotypes often portrayed about each other.

We build and maintain bridges.

We hope this book and resource has been helpful in your consideration and planning. This book and effort is a constant work in progress. As the move towards Africa becomes an increasingly real and permanent option for families and communities of African descent around the globe looking for cultural connectedness, peace of mind, a new experience, retirement or viable investment opportunities, we plan to remain a resource for Ghana and other African countries.

We believe it's more important for those who want to repatriate to Ghana connect and work with someone on the ground with whom they find alignment and trust and more than it is to work with us directly. However, we are available for consultation.

<<<<<<Schedule a consultation with us.
We reserve the right to be selective with whom we choose to work without explanation, reservation or trepidation.

Thank You

We've intentionally connected you with each of our guest contributors directly and sincerely hope you contact them, explore their business products and/or service offerings and patronize them. They are friends and **friendship is essential to the soul**.

Please scan and share your feedback below.

To book the author or carry the book, contact:

Email: booking@theadinkragroup.com

Message Center: +1 240 490 2227

Whatsapp Message: +233 50 436 2582

For Interview Requests:

Email: muhammida@waxprint.media